THE PRICE GUIDE TO ANTIQUE FURNITURE

THE PRICE GUIDE TO ANTIQUE FURNITURE

Edited & Compiled by JOHN ANDREWS

Published by THE ANTIQUE COLLECTORS' CLUB

© Copyright 1969

The copyright of this book is owned jointly by The Antique Collectors' Club and John Andrews.

World copyright reserved

No part of this book may be reproduced in any form without permission from the publisher, except for the quotation of brief passages in criticism.

While every care has been exercised in the compilation of the information contained in this book, neither the author nor the Antique Collectors' Club accept any liability for loss, damage or expense incurred by reliance placed on the information contained in this book.

First printed	November 1968
First reprint	December 1969
Second reprint	January 1969
Third reprint	April 1969
Revised	November 1969
Revised	January 1971

Printed in England by
Baron Publishing, Woodbridge, Suffolk.

DEDICATION

This book is affectionately dedicated to the following people, who were involved, in various ways, in its production:-

       My wife, Geraldine

       John Steel

       Diana Thorpe

       Arthur Chesser

       Joe Hartley

       Derek Green

John Andrews

NEW REFERENCE NUMBERING

Due to the increased number of illustrations, some rearrangement has been necessary in the sequence of pieces originally shown in the 1969 Guide. We have therefore allocated a reference number to each piece so that future Price Revision Lists will have an easy cross reference to the Guide. Owners of the 1969 Price Guide will find that we have shown the original 1969 Guide page number in brackets next to the new reference number. As far as future Revision Lists are concerned, we will quote the reference number of a piece and not its page number.

✲✲✲✲✲✲✲✲✲✲✲

THE ANTIQUE COLLECTORS' CLUB

The Price Guide Series, in whcih this volume was the first, is an off-shoot of the Antique Collectors' Club, which was founded in 1966. Such was, and is, the keenness of almost 7,000 members of the Club to discover more about quality and value of antiques, that the production of this series was undertaken.

The Club magazine, which is sent free to all members, contains four main sections. These are:—

1) News of the activities of the 50 Regional Clubs where members meet to discuss and handle antiques as well as listening to lectures and making visits.
2) Illustrated sale reports showing a selection of the prices realised at auction during the preceding month. Pictures of items sold at auction are so much more illuminating than the mere recital of unillustrated catalogue descriptions and prices.
3) Several liberally illustrated articles each month by practical experts which contain valuable information on prices, price trends, features of value, investment potential, fakes, etc. in fact the information which is essential to the buyer but is not normally covered in commercial magazines on antiques.
4) A large 'For Sale' section through which members buy and sell antiques among themselves. This section has, perhaps, given rise to the myth that the Club is anti-trade. It is not, and this fact is clearly stated in the magazine.

It is the firm belief of all those connected with the running of the Club that the more collectors know about antiques the more enjoyment they will derive, and the more the antique trade in this country will flourish. Accordingly, the magazine regularly carries articles on furniture, not only by the author of the Guide but by many other specialist contributors. A recent development has been the undertaking of original work in the field of Victorian furniture.

The annual subscription of the Antique Collectors' Club is £6.95 per annum.

For Collectors   *By Collectors*   *About Collecting*

The Antique Collectors' Club
Clopton, Woodbridge
Suffolk

ACKNOWLEDGEMENTS

The authors and publishers are deeply indebted to:-

Mr. A.D. Silvester of A.T. Silvester & Sons Ltd. of Solihull who contributed a large number of the illustrations used

Mr. Guy Bousfield of Windsor

Christie, Manson & Woods

Mr. & Mrs. A. Cassidy

Members of the Antique Collectors' Club

for the use of photographs and illustrations in this book.

While to the best of our knowledge the photographs in this publication are the copyright of those who supplied them, we must apologise for any accidental violation of copyright due to changes in ownership.

CONTENTS

	Page
How to use this Guide	1
Some Notes on Antique Furniture	2
Chronology	4
Dictionary of Terminology	7
Chairs	40
Upholstered Chairs	126
Windsor Chairs	150
Dining Tables	161
Side and Card Tables	186
Dressing Tables	223
Pembroke and Sofa Tables	235
Library Tables	249
Tripod Tables	254
Cricket Tables	274
Chests and Chests of Drawers	275
Bureaux	327
Dressers	370
Sideboards and Chiffoniers	385
Corner Cupboards	397
Night Tables	407
Work Tables	414
Canterburies	424
Teapoy	429
Washstands	432
Cellaret or Wine Cooler	433
Dough Bin	434
Whatnot	435
Toilet Mirrors	436
Knife Boxes	443

PREFACE - PRICE BASIS

How is it possible to quote price ranges for pieces of antique furniture? The willingness of the seller to part with a piece and the eagerness of the buyer to acquire it must cause fundamental variations to occur in price. This is only the start of the problem, for there are an infinite number of permutations in the features affecting the price of an antique. Some features were incorporated by the makers, others have occured by sheer accident of time.

When this publication was mooted by the author, the publishers posed this, among many other objections. It was only after the author had predicted, within reasonable bounds, the prices which would be asked in a variety of shops for the more common pieces that the possibility of the project was accepted.

Such would not have been the case some time ago. It was then accepted that one went into the country areas to buy cheaply. While this practice is still prevalent, a gradual standardisation in price occured, particularly in the better provincial shops. While the increase in demand and the rapid dissemination of knowledge about antiques help to explain this standardisation of price, there are two additional factors which have assured it. The first is the countrywide scouring by overseas buyers in search of general items and the second is the proliferation of localised antique fairs within the last two or three years. These fairs are attended by many dealers who are in regular circulation. Were these factors not sufficient, the improvement of transport has enabled many town dealers to use much wider catchment areas.

Given that a standardisation of price is occurring, which price should be quoted in such a guide? Auction prices are immediately attractive, as prices obtained in the open market would seem to be a reliable reflection of demand. One has, however, only to study the prices obtained at auction to see the extreme variations which can occur between the restraint of professional presence and the exuberance and near-mania resulting from competition between private buyers.

Another method which recommended itself was to record pieces in shops. Here again however, the extreme variations between fashionable shops in high rent areas and near junk-shops, from whom the former obtain their supplies, confused any categorisation.

What basis therefore has been used? The prices given in this guide are those which have been noted as available to collectors who are prepared to make some effort to obtain the pieces described. On the whole they reflect the prices of the better provincial and suburban shops where good value for money can be obtained. It is not the object of this book to cover the exceptional pieces dealt with by the London West End Specialists. Anyone wishing to follow the pricing of such pieces could usefully also subscribe to the catalogues and price lists of the leading auctioneers.

It is not therefore implied that it would be foolhardy to pay more than the top of the price range indicated for a piece. The buyer must, however, be aware that he is paying a premium for a particular piece if he does this. We hope that this book will bring this awareness to him. Where the price paid is lower than the bottom of the range quoted the buyer should pay particular attention to ensure that he is really obtaining a bargain.

Price apart, we believe that this book will enable the reader to make a more practical assessment of the antique furniture available today than the purely historically based anthologies of museum and other unobtainable pieces normally presented by the authors and publishers concerned to illustrate the highest recorded craftsmanship.

HOW TO USE THIS GUIDE

The price ranges shown are an indication to private individuals of what should be obtainable. Where prices asked by dealers are substantially different, no useful purpose is served by commenting on the fact. It is well known that the return on capital employed in the antique trade is relatively low. In order to maintain the kind of stock for which he has built up a reputation, a dealer may be forced to purchase at higher prices than those envisaged at time of publication due to vagaries of local supply and demand. One of the most renowned features of the established members of the antique trade is their unfailing courtesy and consideration. It is not the object of this publication to disparage individual dealers prices. Without the existence of such dealers antique collecting would be well-nigh impossible.

The price brackets quoted are designed to cover the pieces illustrated. The position of a piece within the brackets can be further defined by the possession of 'value points' sometimes shown. These are defined as follows:-

+ a minor feature which influences prices to a degree affected by a number of other features, particularly of higher value.
++ a feature of some importance in placing the piece within the price bracket, also affected by other features of higher value.
+++ a feature which places the piece towards the top of the brackets.
++++ a feature which lifts the piece over the top of the range, often by a significant amount.

The pieces are listed by type in chronological order for convenience. In this way we hope that the book will provide a useful sequence for collectors to distinguish periods of English furniture. As such we believe it will take its place as a complementary publication to standard text books on the subject, recommended below:-

English Furniture	John C. Rogers
English Period Furniture	A. Hayward
Antique Collectors' Club	1st & 2nd Year Books
Shorter Dictionary of English Furniture	Ralph Edwards

SOME NOTES ON ANTIQUE FURNITURE

Of all the antiques collected by individuals none can give more enjoyment or exasperation than furniture. Craftsmanship in wood for a utilitarian and decorative purpose probably presents the greatest appeal to the artistic appreciation of the widest range of people. The only concern which modifies the acquisition of antique pieces is the question of originality.

In the early nineteenth century and before there were probably no more than ten million people living in these islands, most of them extremely poor. The rise in the middle classes in the late Georgian period undoubtedly caused large quantities of furniture to be made but it is as well to bear in mind that it was for a minority. For the last sixty years, starting with oak and gaining speed rapidly through successive periods, antique English furniture has been avidly collected, not only by British, but by worldwide acquirers as well. Vast quantities have been exported never to return; to this must be added the annual loss by fire, damage and final wear.

The enormous trade in antiques and the high quality restorers available have meant that very few pieces neglected in house, cottage and barn have not been looked over at some time by a professional with a view to profit. Bargains are, therefore, scarce but fortunately this has been compensated for in recent years by the steep rise in prices. It is accepted that the high price of today is the bargain of tomorrow. Due to this scarcity and widespread demand there is an extra factor which complicates the position; the creation of 'antiques' which are, in fact, new. Many of these expertly made of old wood, were never intended to be anything but genuine 'old' reproductions or marriages of similar broken pieces to make one sound one. With the passage of time, however, they have been assumed, mistakenly often enough, to be original. Many were created for an export trade and few dealers fail to point out what they are. Some, however, are slowly absorbed into the system and become accepted. It is no longer possible for any but the richest collectors to demand entirely original, top quality pieces, which must practically have a provenance. Ordinary furniture over the years must become used, damaged, repaired and polished. With the acceptance of this has come an acceptance of what sometimes are alterations, mellowed by time and difficult to distinguish. We are now reaching a situation where there is comparatively little original furniture of the eighteenth century, or before, left. For this reason, quite apart from disastrous economic situations, prices are rising and originality is at a premium.

On the other side of the picture, however, there is no doubt that many beginners in furniture collecting are unrealistic. There is no longer quite the faddism about freedom from worm which was once so prevalent but many collectors are still over-concerned about small repairs and repolished surfaces. Although it is obvious that all now deplore the French polishing of antique pieces, the wear and tear of years can cause something rather nastily removed from mellow patination which may require surface treatment. Drastic restoration is perhaps an unfortunate necessity which detracts from the price involved but which preserves the piece. Indeed very few pieces of furniture would now be left available were it not for the skill of our craftsmen over a long period. It is only when restoration has been done with a view to structural alteration and 'improvement' that objections become valid. The collector must, therefore, be prepared to accept a certain amount of restoration whilst assessing its overall effect on the price of a piece accordingly.

CHRONOLOGY

Monarch	Date of Reign	Period Appelation	Publications and Events
James I	1603 – 1625	Jacobean	
Charles I	1625 – 1649	Carolean	
Commonwealth	1649 – 1660	Cromwellian or Commonwealth	
Charles II	1660 – 1685	Restoration	
James II	1685 – 1689	Restoration	
William & Mary	1689 – 1694	William & Mary	
William III	1694 – 1702	William III or William & Mary	
Anne	1702 – 1714	Queen Anne	
George I	1714 – 1727	George I - early Georgian	
George II	1727 – 1760	Early Georgian	1754 Robert Adam b. 1728 d. 1792. T. Chippendale 'Gentleman and Cabinet Maker's Director'. 1st Ed.
George III	1760 – 1811	Later Georgian	1763 Ince and Mayhew 'System of Household Furniture'.
			1766 R. Manwaring 'Chairmaker's Guide'.
			1788 A. Hepplewhite 'Cabinet Maker's and Upholsterer's Guide'. 1st Ed.
			1791 Thomas Sheraton 'Cabinet Maker's and Upholsterer's Drawing Book', 1st Ed.

George III (Regency)	1811 – 1820	Regency	1807	Thomas Hope 'Household Furniture'.	
			1808	George Smith 'Household Furniture'.	
George IV	1820 – 1830	Regency			
William IV	1830 – 1837	Late Regency or William IV			
Victoria	1837 – 1901	Early Victorian up to 1860 Later Victorian 1860 – 1901			
Edward VII	1901 – 1910	Edwardian			

PRICE REVISION LISTS

1st JULY   **1st JANUARY**

The usefulness of a book containing prices rapidly diminishes as market values change, for prices can fall as well as rise.

In order to keep the prices in this book fully up-dated a revised price list will be issued on 1st July and 1st December each year. These lists will contain the current values of all the pieces illustrated in the book.

To ensure that you receive the Price Revision Lists twice yearly, complete the banker's order form and send it to the Antique Collectors' Club now.

Price revision lists cost £1.00 each, or £2.00 a year by banker's order, from:—

THE ANTIQUE COLLECTORS' CLUB, CLOPTON, WOODBRIDGE, SUFFOLK.

DICTIONARY OF TERMINOLOGY

Acanthus
A leaf design used to ornament furniture in carving. Although used earlier it is most frequently found in mahogany furniture from 1730 and continued to be popular among Victorians.

Adam, Robert
See "Styles".

Amorini
Cupids or boys used in decoration. Popular in the late seventeenth and early eighteenth century viz. 'boyes and crownes' design spandrels on clock faces. Also used in Adam designs. See chair C1008.

Anthemian
Another decoration, this time like the flower of the honeysuckle. Again used in Adam designs and also during the Regency period.

Arcaded Decoration
A series of arches on pillars or columns.

Art Nouveau
A style of the late Victorian and Edwardian period. The furniture was generally tall and narrow and the heart-shape much used as decoration. See "Styles".

Astragal
A moulding used on glazing bars of bookcases.

Ball and Claw
A foot design used for legs of furniture from c.1710. See "Cabriole Leg".

Baluster
A turned shaping used on legs of furniture or centre columns. Usually rather bulbous but also in modified forms.

Bamboo Turning
A simulated bamboo shaping on legs of furniture dating from late eighteenth century. See Work Table WT 1784

Banding
Used around the edges of tables or drawers for decorative effect, the art and proportion of the banding is vital to the success of the design. Straight banding is one which has been cut along the grain: crossbanding describes that where the

7

wood has been cut across the grain. Very decorative effects were obtained by using different and exotic woods for crossbanding. Herringbone or feather bandings were used in walnut furniture — see drawer fronts under "Drawer" section.

Barley-Sugar Twist See "Spiral Twist".

Baroque See "Styles".

Bead Mould Used for two types of moulding: either a small plain moulding of semi-circular section or one in the form of a string of beads.

Bearer The rectangular section length of wood under a bureau fall which pulls out to support the fall when open. Many a fall has been smashed off its hinges by people forgetting to pull out the bearers before opening the fall.

Bentwood Type of furniture exhibited at 1851 Exhibition by Michael Thonet, an Austrian. Generally made from birch bent and curved by means of steam heating to form graceful shapes. See chair Reference No. UC1118.

Bergere An armchair, originally with upholstered sides but now a term used to describe a chair with carved sides and back, generally post-1800 in date. See chair section UC1111 - UC1112.

Bird-Cage Gallery A construction used under the top of a tripod table to enable it to revolve as well as tip up. Formed by two squares of wood with four turned columns between, pivoting about the centre column. See Reference No. TT1384.

Blind Fret Fretwork glued or carved upon a solid surface. See "Frets".

Bobbin Turning Turning of baluster in shape of bobbins, one on top of another.

Boulle A form of marquetry made from shell and metal named after Andre Charles Boulle, a French artist of the Louis XIV period. Boulle (or Buhl) furniture was also popular in the Regency period in England,

	but it is thought that the English marquetry of the William and Mary period was influenced by the French Boulle designs.
Boulton, Matthew	Famous for his collaboration with James Watt on the steam engine, but his Birmingham foundry also produced metal ormolu mounts for furniture from 1762.
Bow-front Chest	See Chest section, references CH1439/1440/1441.
Bracket Foot	A type of foot for chests, bureaux and cabinets introduced c.1690. The outside bracket shape does not in fact support the weight of the piece which is taken on a wood block under the corner of the carcase on to which the shaped outside bracket fits.
Brass Stringing	Particularly popular on chairs and tables of the late Georgian and Regency period. Usually a mark of quality and certainly influential in raising the price of a piece.
Break-front	A term usually applied to bookcases and descriptive of a centre section which protrudes out beyond the line of the sides.
Broken Pediment	A pediment above a piece of furniture which is usually classical in style with, of course, the centre point missing i.e. 'broken'. Used particularly above bureau bookcases of the first half of the eighteenth century in both walnut and mahogany examples. See references B1506/1526 for illustrations.
Bulb	The bulging or bulbous turned part of supports or legs of early furniture of the oak period i.e. before c.1650. Also seen in later seventeenth century walnut turning. See chair Reference C1012.
Buffet	A term loosely used to describe a piece of furniture of the sixteenth and seventeenth century used as a sideboard, with open shelves supported on bulbous turned members.
Bun Foot	A turned ball-shaped foot of flattened form, like a cheese, used from c.1650 - 1710 particularly on chests and bureaux. The spigot by which the bun

foot was attached to the piece was often turned with a coarse worn thread which matched that of the socket (under the corner of the piece) into which it fitted. See Reference No. CH1410

Bureau See Section 10.

Bureau-Bookcase See Section 10.

Cabinet Makers Furniture was originally made by 'joiners' but from the end of the seventeenth century trades became more specific. The advent of the finer quality work of the William and Mary period and particularly the cabinet work involved gave rise to the term 'cabinet maker' who was generally specified as the maker of chests, bureaux and bookcases, whereas tables and stands were still made by a joiner. However, during the eighteenth century the masters of workshops started to call themselves 'cabinet makers' rather than joiners. The most famous names now associated with the eighteenth century are Chippendale, Hepplewhite and Sheraton — see under "Styles" — but some of the more celebrated of their time were:-

Cobb, John. With his partner, **William Vile**, the firm of Vile and Cobb were probably the most celebrated in the period 1755 - 65. They were cabinet makers and upholsterers to George III and pieces made by them remain in the Royal Collection. Cobb was originally the upholsterer until Vile's retirement in 1765.

Copland, M. A. furniture designer who, with **Matthois Lock** published designs in a book 'A New Book of Ornaments in 1746'. It is thought that since Lock and Copland worked for Chippendale, the latter used their designs for his famous 'Director' on which his reputation has been made.

Gillow, Robert. Came from Lancaster where the furniture for the London branch in Oxford Street was made. The firm of Gillow's of Lancaster was in business in the mid-eighteenth century (Hepplewhite was a **Gillow** apprentice) and continued on throughout the nineteenth. The firm's Cost Books from about 1790 with designs are to be seen in the Westminster Public Library.

Haigh, Thomas. Was a partner of both father and son Chippendales.

Ince, William.. Partner in the firm of Ince and Mayhew which was a firm of high reputation and who published a book of designs, the 'Universal System of Household Furniture' 1759 - 63. The firm continued to produce into the early part of the nineteenth century.

Langley, Batty and Thomas. Produced a book, 'The City and Country Builders and Workman's Treasury of Designs', in 1740, a manual for craftsmen containing mainly architectural designs in the prevailing taste.

Langlois, Peter. A cabinet maker who supplied furniture for Strawberry Hill and Syon House, 1760 - 70 and who worked a great deal in the Boulle (g.v.) manner.

Lock, Matthois.. Lock and Copland produced 'A New Book of Ornaments, etc.' in 1740 and it is said that Chippendale organised much of their work, since they were employed by him.

Manwaring, Robert.. Published another book of designs in 1765. 'The Cabinet and Chair Maker's Real Friend and Companion', containing many designs for chairs, some of them rather clumsy.

Mayhew, Thomas. Partner in the firm of Ince and Mayhew. See under Ince.

Seddon, George. (1727 - 1801). A cabinet maker whose firm was large and which covered nearly all trades.

Shearer, Thomas. Cabinet maker and author of 'Designs for Household Furniture' 1788.

Smith, George. Cabinet maker and author of 'A Collection of Designs for Household Furniture and Interior Decoration', 1808.

Vile, William. Senior partner in the firm of Vile and Cobb, probably the most famous of the period 1755 - 65. See also Cobb.

Cabochon A design motif found often on the knees of chairs of the early mahogany period — c.1740 consisting of a ball shape usually surrounded by leaf ornament.

Cabriole Leg See illustrations of chairs references C1013 and C1015. Introduced to England in the early eighteenth century and originally terminating in a hoof foot, the cabriole leg was subject to many design variations and was produced with pad, hoof, claw and ball, paw and scroll foot according to taste. The design seems to have declined after 1750 until early Victorian times, when it was revived.

Caning First used in chairs in the mid-seventeenth century i.e. at the Restoration or Charles II period. Its use seems to have declined after the William and Mary period (1689 - 1702) and was revived again in the late eighteenth century. Hepplewhite and Shearer both illustrated carved chairs in the 1790's and subsequently, through Regency and Victorian periods, it was used in dining chairs and others. See references C1006, 1007, 1013, 1065 and 1066: UC1111, 1112

Canterbury A term used in the late eighteenth century for rather mobile furniture and said to be named after an Archbishop of that See. Sheraton illustrated a 'supper Canterbury' which was the forerunner of the modern tea trolley, used for holding cutlery and plates. Music Canterburys were produced from the late eighteenth century and through the nineteenth in contemporary styles. See section 18.

Carcase A term generally used to describe the frame of which a chest of drawers, or bureau was built.

Cartouche A decoration, usually in the form of a flat surface with shield or scroll shape on which an inscription or monogram can be placed.

Caryatid A carved female figure used as decoration or support i.e. a leg, on furniture of the early seventeenth century or again after 1800.

Casters	Early forms of casters were made – c.1700 – of wood, both wheel and axle. In the mid-eighteenth century leather rollers appear to have come in use but in the last quarter of the century brass casters with stylised motifs made their appearance. See Table Sections for typical examples.
Cavetto	A hollowed, concave moulding of quarter-circle section. See "Mouldings".
Chamfer	A bevelled edge used to lighten the effect of a piece of furniture. Used on legs of 'Chippendale' type – see tables, Reference No's. ST1271, S1273 and chairs – see C1031. Also a design feature of top halves of tallboys – see CH1421, 1434, B1511 and mahogany chests – see CH1431.
Chairs	See Section 1
Chests	See Section 9
Chiffonier	See Section 12
Chippendale	See "Styles"
Clay, Henry	Originator of papier mache furniture, about 1772. Made by building up layers of paper with pitch and oil over an iron frame. Usually finished by painting and decorating with inlay.
Clubfoot	Virtually the same as a pad-foot and most commonly found on cabriole legs. See "Pad foot".
Clustered Column	A design of medieval origin used in the mid-eighteenth century consisting of several pillars clustered together. See chair, Reference No. UC1104.
Cock Bead	A small round bead moulding used on the edges of drawer fronts from 1725-1800.
Column Turning	Turning in the form of a column used from the mid-seventeenth century onwards. See gate-leg table, Reference No. DT1205.
Commode	A term borrowed from France and used from the mid-eighteenth century to describe a piece of

furniture for use in principal rooms. Very fine examples in Adam or prevailing styles with rounded or serpentine shaped fronts, and original French pieces, resembling finely decorated chests of drawers, with or without doors; represent the height of collecting, in both taste and purse. A term which should not be used as a Victorian euphemism for a piece of furniture designed to conceal a chamber pot.

Console Table   A wall side table supported by brackets.

Cross-banding   See "Banding".

Cushion Drawer   A drawer set in the upper moulding or frieze of a secretaire or chest having a convex, or 'cushion', shape to the front. See Reference No.B1508.

Davenport   See Reference No. B1535 et seq.

Dentil Frieze   The part of a frieze moulding of dentillated or 'square-toothed' form. Made up of a series of small rectangular blocks. See "Mouldings".

Diaper   A decorative pattern of diamond-shaped lines with dots or forms inside. Used for border decoration.

Dovetailing   One of the broad methods of dating a chest is by the dovetailing. In sixteenth and early seventeenth century pieces the drawer sides were nailed into a rebated front as shown on photograph 1. During the first half of the seventeenth century however, fairly crude dovetails were introduced as shown in photograph 2. Note that both these drawers have side runners, i.e. a groove let in to the thick side linings, made of oak, acts as a bearing for rectangular section bearers inside the carcase, on which the drawer runs and is supported.

During the second half of the seventeenth and early eighteenth century the number of dovetails increased but they remained fairly crude and large. See photograph 3. By the time the mahogany period was in full swing, after 1740, the dovetails had increased further and become finer. See photograph 4. This form has continued up to modern times.

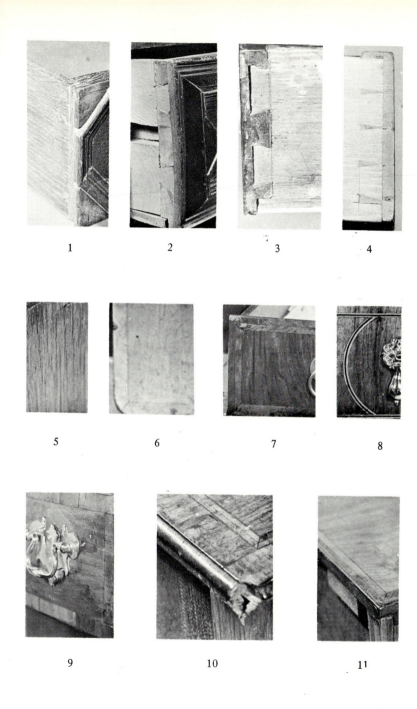

Dough Bin   See Reference No. DB1840.

Dowel   A wooden peg used to fasten timber joints.

Drawers   A guide to dating furniture with drawers can be obtained from their construction. On the chests of the early seventeenth century the drawers were nailed together, with the side linings rebated into the front, as shown in Photograph 1 under the heading "Dovetails". Subsequently dovetails were used as shown in photograph 2 of that section. The weight of the drawers was taken on side runners which fitted into grooves cut in the thick sides of the drawer. This is also evident in photograph 2.

About the time of the transition to walnut, in 1680, the bottom runner appeared. This was a strip of wood — usually oak — fixed under the drawer at each end which ran on horizontal bearers on the interlinings of a chest. The drawer bottom, whether of pine or oak, ran from front to back as far as grain was concerned, as shown in photograph 5. Between the drawer fronts the carcase face was flat.

However, when the change to veneered walnut furniture took place, a variety of possibilities came about. Initially it is probable that a vertically veneered front with simple diagonal grain cross-banding — a sort of half herringbone — was used, as shown in photograph 6. This was in use from c. 1680 to c. 1710. However, herringbone cross-banding, as shown in photograph 7, was used from c. 1690 to c. 1720 and probably was more common. A variation was the use of inlaid boxwood and ebony stringing lines from c. 1690 to c. 1710, as shown in photograph 8.

Between the drawers at this time the carcase fronts were covered by the half-round or 'D' moulding and the double half-round or double 'D' moulding, with the latter the rarer of the two.

Usually double 'D' moulding, cut, like the single version, across the grain, was used to maintain the proportion on broader carcase front edgings. A country form of simple cross-banding to drawers was used, with the half herringbone, well into the first half of the eighteenth century and is shown in photograph 9.

About 1710 an alternative form appeared. This was the drawer edged by an ovolo lip moulding which hid the gap between the drawer and the carcase edge. The carcase front edging was, in this case, flat veneered, obviating the need for 'D' or double 'D' mouldings. A disadvantage was that unless the stop blocks at the back of the drawer remained fixed, it was possible to break off the lip moulding by pushing the drawer in too hard. This is shown in photograph 10.

Concurrent with the lip moulding the cock bead appeared. This is generally assumed to have been widely adopted about 1730 and the walnut drawer front of photograph 11 with its herringbone banding is of about this date. The cock bead solved the lip moulding breakage problem and was used on mahogany furniture from 1730 throughout the eighteenth and nineteenth century, although plain mahogany drawers without any beading were also common.

The linings used continued to be oak or pine and in later furniture, from about 1770, the bottom was made with the grain running across instead of front to back. About 1790 some drawer bottoms had a central bearer introduced and were made in two halves running across again. This continued up to the present day.

Dressers	See Section 11.
Dressing Tables	See Section 5.
Dumb Waiters	See Reference No. **TT1390**

Eagles' Heads	A form of decoration used particularly in the early mahogany period. See chair, Reference No. C1019.
Ebonized Wood	Wood which has been stained black to simulate ebony.
Escritoire	A word borrowed from the French to denote a piece of furniture at which one can write. Synonym of secretaire.
Escutcheon	A motif used as a centre decoration.
Fielded Panel	A panel which has the edges bevelled or chamfered. See chests, Reference No.'s. CH1406, CH1410.
Finial	A turned knob used at the intersection of stretchers on tables, chairs and stools to complete a design effect. Also used on the hoods of longcase clocks.
Fluting	Grooving of semi-circular or concave section used, usually vertically, as ornament or design to give a lightening effect. See chests, Reference No's. CH1431, B2511.
Frets	Fretwork either applied or cut from solid and used as decoration. If presented on a solid surface, known as a 'blind' fret. If left as open decoration, known as 'open' fret. Used particularly in mid- and later eighteenth century in Gothic or Chinese taste. See chair, Reference No. C1026, card table, ST1273, chests, CH1432, 1435.
Frieze	The surface below a table top or the part of a cornice consisting of the flat surface beneath the top moulding. See Reference No. M1435 for typical example.
Gadrooning	A carved edge of repetitive shapes usually convex curved form. Shown well on card table frieze Reference No. ST1272. See also "Mouldings".
Gallery	A decorative metal border, usually brass.

Gesso   A plaster composition, white in colour, used as a base for applying gilding.

Gillows   See "Cabinet Makers".

Gothic   See "Styles".

Handles   Funnily enough, wooden knobs were used on drawer furniture in the seventeenth century oak period until about 1660, when brass drops were introduced. Funnily, because one always associates wooden knobs with Victorians. However, brass drops rapidly came in to use and oak and walnut furniture of the 1660 - 1710 period is usually found to have drops similar to those shown in photographs 12 and 13. The handle on these pulls was linked to a double strip of brass or iron which passed through the drawer front and was then parted and turned over so that each end was pinned to the drawer back in opposing vertical senses. Modern reproductions have a threaded spigot with a nut to secure it.

From about 1690, however, the brass loop handle with solid back plate appeared, as shown in photographs 14 and 15. The back plate was shaped and could be engraved, as in photograph 15, and the loop was cast and perhaps moulded, as in photograph 14. Brass knob-shaped sockets on the face of bolts held the loop ends.

Pierced back plates were introduced about 1710 and showed many forms of which photographs 16 and 17 are but two examples. Both walnut and later mahogany furniture used the solid and pierced back plate, but by 1740 the 'swan-neck', which is often associated with cock beaded drawers, had been introduced. This is shown in photograph 18. In this type the loop is thicker and there are merely two metal moulded circular roses behind each bolt head, without any back plate. It was a type capable of considerable ornamentation as

 (12)
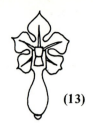 (13)
 (19)
 (14)
 (20)
 (15)
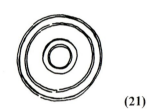 (21)
 (16)
 (22)
 (17)
 (23)
 (18)

shown in photograph 19 and the later fine quality pieces — after 1750 — had very Rococo forms of this in cast and chased metal of a type found on commodes — see Reference No. CH1432.

About 1780 the stamped brass back plate of oval or circular form associated with Hepplewhite or Sheraton furniture came into use. Photograph 20 is a typical example. This would be made from thin sheet brass, stamped to shape and hence hollow at the back.

About 1800 the turned wooden knob — photograph 21 — came in to use and, although there was a period of overlap, by the time the Victorian period had set in, most drawer furniture used wooden knobs of varied simplicity or complication. Some had a simple wooden spigot to fit into the drawer front; some had a wooden threaded screwed spigot; some had a metal bolt set into them. Unfortunately the Victorians considered that the wooden knob was so desirable that they could not resist fitting it to furniture from other periods with the result that walnut and early mahogany chests in thousands have been despoiled by Victorian 'improvers'.

With the return of eighteenth century fashions, from about 1880 onwards it was necessary to return to brass handles again, although wooden knobs continued to be fitted to ordinary furniture. Photograph 22 shows a late Victorian version of a brass loop and back plate fitted to a 'reproduction' of an eighteenth century piece. Photograph 23 shows an Edwardian Art Nouveau handle and stamped back plate as fitted to the 'simple' furniture of the period which strived to return to medieval simplicity of line!

For further details the Chest and Chest of Drawers section shows typical period handles.

Hepplewhite   See "Styles".

Herringbone	An inlaid banding or border used in walnut veneered furniture for decorative effect. Also called 'feather-banding'. Made by laying two strips of veneer at right angles to each other in 'V' form to give a feathered or herringbone effect.
Hipping	A form of cabriole leg extension used on rather better quality pieces, in which the leg continues at the top to a level above the seat rail.
Hoof foot	An animal form of foot used on early, perhaps original, cabriole legs. The French name was pied-de-biche. See Reference No. C1013.
Hope, Thomas	Scholar and architect who published a book 'Household Furniture and Decoration' in 1807. His designs were of formalised classical type with much zoological decoration and drew on nearly all the ancient civilizations for their forms.
Husk	A decoration used in Adam and Hepplewhite designs of bell-shaped form frequently shown in festoons.
Ince and Mayhew	See "Cabinet Makers".
Inlay	A decoration which has been let into the solid wood. Used from mid-sixteenth century onwards.
Japanning	Another term for lacquering (q.v.).
Kent, William	See "Styles".
Lacquer	Lacquer furniture was popular from an early date, being originally imported during the sixteenth century but becoming more popular during the seventeenth. By the late seventeenth century it was being produced in England, but the vogue seemed to die down to lesser proportions in the second quarter of the eighteenth century. Nevertheless lacquering continued to be used as decoration into the nineteenth century.
Langlois, Peter	See "Cabinet Makers".

Linenfold	A carving design used on panels of early sixteenth century date.
Linings	The interior parts of a drawer.
Lion Mask	A decoration of carved form popular in the early mahogany period — 1720 - 40 and again in the Regency period.
Lock and Copland	See "Cabinet Makers".
Lowboy	A term, probably of American origin, now used to describe a dressing table or side table usually on cabriole legs.
Manwaring	See "Cabinet Makers."
Marquetry	Veneers of different woods cut into designs and fitted together to give a decorative effect. To be distinguished from inlays (q.v.) by the fact that design is veneered on to a carcase and not cut into the solid. See chest: reference No. CH1413.
Mirrors, Toilet	See section 21.
Mitre Joint	A joint made by fitting together two surfaces cut at an angle of 45°.
Monopodium	A carved support with a lion-mask top. The foot is usually of claw form and this type of support is of Regency period.
Mouldings	In the last analysis, perhaps the most important features which date a piece of furniture are its mouldings. More correctly, they are often the factor which ultimately determines its originality and the extent to which it has been restored or 'improved' with a view to pre-dating or faking a later piece. In the eighteenth century and before, the mouldings used were based on architectural designs and had a boldness of shape and execution which nineteenth century makers with machines to do the work, failed to maintain. The meanness and over-sophistication of the mouldings on Victorian reproductions gives them away instantly,

quite apart from considerations of colour and ageing.

Mouldings of the oak period were bold and generally cut along the grain. It was in the walnut period that the cross-grained mouldings in small pieces, which generally shrink slightly apart and yellow so beautifully with age, came into their own. On the best walnut furniture the mouldings were always cut across the grain, although those along the sides of a piece of furniture might be cut along the grain on lesser quality pieces to save time and money. In mahogany furniture the applied mouldings are nearly always cut along the grain. Integral mouldings, of course, cut across.

Towards the end of the eighteenth century the mouldings became tighter and under the influence of Hepplewhite and Sheraton designs were curtailed or dispensed with altogether. Carcase edges were flat veneered, as were projecting edges.

In the sketch illustrations we have shown a few of the principal types. Photograph 24 shows a thumbnail edge moulding of a type used on chests and other furniture from c.1650 to c.1720. This was obviously capable of development and photograph 25 shows a more sophisticated form used from c.1720 to c.1760. The use of a 'cavetto' or concave form of cornice moulding started c.1690 and photograph 26 shows one of the basic forms. About the turn of the century, c.1700 and onwards, the architectural influence, as exemplified by William Kent c.1715 — see "Styles" — became very strong and many mouldings followed quite simply the orders of the Palladian School. For instance photograph 27, a cornice moulding of the 1690 - 1730 period is a composite form of pedestal cap, whereas photograph 28, with a dentil course, is a variation of this used c.1745.

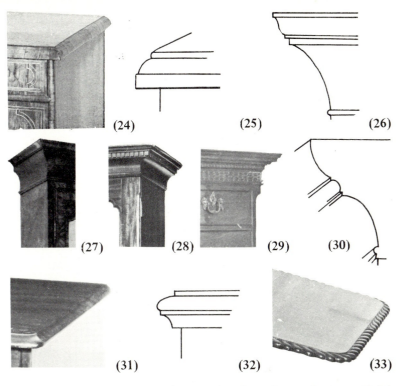

(24) (25) (26) (27) (28) (29) (30) (31) (32) (33)

Quartering – *A walnut dower chest on cabriole legged stand with shell carving on the knee and apron. The front shows the effect of 'quartering', i.e. laying four sheets of veneer with identical figure in opposing senses to give a formal pattern. The chest also shows ball and claw feet and 'herringbone' or 'feather' inlay.*

(34)

A more elaborate form, with heavier proportion in the top moulding above the dentil course is shown in photograph 29, a moulding to be found on cornices of rather lavish furniture of c.1750. Gradually, however, these cornice mouldings were altered and by 1795 one has the combination form of photograph 30 which is a cavetto combined with a reverse top curve.

Another form, found on cornices of the 1780 - 90 period is shown in the photograph. This is an arcaded cavetto which has been sophisticated by the addition of a dentil course above the arcading.

The top edge mouldings of chests were also capable of sophistication, although the rather simple curve of photograph 31 is probably the one most found on chests of the early mahogany period. Chest CH1431 exhibits this feature. It was, however, used from 1720 to 1780. A simple form of half-round top edge moulding was also in use from the mid-seventeenth century onwards, but in later and more elaborate furniture of the c.1745 period it was often carved with riband and rosette form, which was popular from this time up to the late eighteenth century.

Another top edge moulding of c.1750 date is shown in photograph 32 where a combination of thumb-nail and concave mouldings has been used.

Photograph 33 shows a gadrooned edge, which came into use about 1740 and continued as a decorative form on into the nineteenth century.

Ogee   A double curve, convex at the top and turning to concave below.

Open Fret	See "Frets."
Ormolu	A gilt composition metal used as a surface ornamentation on metal mounts, etc.
Ovolo	A moulding form of a convex quarter-circle section. Used around drawer edges to lip over carcase fronts in walnut and early mahogany furniture up to c.1745.
Oyster Veneer	Oystershell veneering, or parquetry work, was produced by cutting the small branches of walnut, laburnum, olive and other woods across the branch to give a concentric ringed effect and laying these veneers in a decorative pattern. The form was introduced from Holland in the late seventeenth century — see chests Reference No's. CH1415, CH1416.
Pad Foot	A round foot at the base of a cabriole or straighter turned leg. See tables Reference No. ST1264 — 7.
Parquetry	A geometric pattern of veneers, often oysters, usually involving stringing and inlays. Contemporary with marquetry.
Patera	A round or oval decoration either applied, carved or painted on wood, used as an ornament.
Patina	The deep surface shine or gloss produced by years of undisturbed polishing and rubbing.
Paw Foot	A foot design used on cabriole legs in the mid-eighteenth century.
Pediment	A moulding or shape above the cornice of bookcases and other furniture. See "Broken Pediment".
Pie-crust	An edge carving of scalloped form used in the later eighteenth century, particularly on tea and tripod tables. See Reference No. TT1383.
Plinth	The square base of a column; also used to describe the flat base support of a piece of furniture.
Polishing	In the seventeenth century it seems to have been the practice to polish oak furniture by means of

rubbing in poppy or linseed oil, often dyed with alkanet root. Subsequently beeswax and turpentine polish was used to keep surfaces in good condition and to preserve the wood.

Walnut furniture of the late seventeenth and early eighteenth century was initially brushed with oil varnish to provide a surface for polishing with wax. The retention of this oil varnish, which provides a magnificently mellowed surface after years of polishing is an important factor in patination.

Mahogany furniture of the eighteenth century was treated according to its type. Spanish or Cuban mahogany was either rubbed with linseed oil or wax and often stained with alkanet root or some other dye to obtain the red colour then very popular. Indeed, oak and walnut furniture of this period was also stained this way. Honduras mahogany was either oil varnished or rubbed with linseed oil and brick dust to give a hard polish. Domestically it seems to have been common to oil furniture, but beeswax polishing with a brush was employed also.

About 1810 the process of French polishing began by using shellac dissolved in spirit. This helped to seal off the wood and provide a bright hard finish. French polishing has developed much since then and is now a much shorter process than the original method. Nearly all furniture was French polished during the nineteenth century and few pieces from the eighteenth century have survived in an unstripped repolished condition. Varnishing in the modern sense was also used, many inferior woods being varnished dark brown in order to resemble mahogany.

Quartering A means of obtaining a formal pattern in wood figure by taking four consecutively cut pieces of veneer, which have identical figuring, and setting them in opposing senses to give a mirrored pattern effect. Used in the walnut period 1680 - 1730 for tops of tables chests and door fronts. See photograph 34.

Rails The horizontal part of a joined frame of a panelled piece of furniture. See "Chests". Also: Top Rail or Cresting Rail — used to describe the top wooden member between the uprights of a chair back.

Ram's Head Decoration used by Adam in mask form.

Reeding Convex raised beads on furniture: the opposite of fluting. Used on eighteenth century furniture and particularly later eighteenth and nineteenth century chair and table legs. See Reference No. C1080.

Rococo See "Styles".

Rule Joint An edge joint found on drop-flap tables from the seventeenth century, but pretty well superseding other plain joints in the eighteenth century. Used on gate-leg and Pembroke tables.

Runner The strip of wood on which a drawer runs.

Scagliola A plaster and marble chip composition, made to imitate marble, used for table tops in the eighteenth century.

Scroll Foot A cabriole leg termination of French origin used from mid-eighteenth century date. See Reference No. C1076.

Scrutoir Synonym for escritoire, secretaire or writing cabinet.

Serpentine A curved shaping particularly valued in chest front forms. See chest Reference No. CH1432.

Shell The shell, or scallop, was a popular decorative motif in the walnut and early mahogany period, covering the years from 1700 up to c.1770. See photograph 34 of chest under heading "quartering".

Spade Foot	A tapered foot of square section used in the later eighteenth century and much associated with Sheraton and Hepplewhite designs. See chairs Reference No's. C1048, 1049.
Spandrel	A decoration used in square corners, usually on clock dials to fill the space between curved chapter ring and the corners.
Spiral Twist	A form of turning used on legs of the late seventeenth century, particularly on tables and stands. Also used on chairs. Particularly popular at the Restoration c.1670. See Reference No's. C1004 1006 for chairs, ST1252 for table and CH1413 for chest.
Splat	The vertical central upright of a chair back. It can be solid or pierced, plain or carved.
Split Baluster	Used as a decoration on chests of sixteenth and seventeenth century and made by splitting a turned baluster vertically in half to provide a flat surface for application. See chests, Reference No's. CH1405, 1409 and dresser D1601.
Spoon-back	Descriptive of chair back on which the splat curves like a spoon handle. See chair Reference No. C1014.
Stile	The vertical part of framing of a panelled piece of furniture. See chest Reference No. CH1402.
Strapwork	Carved decoration used originally in the oak period from mid-sixteenth to mid-seventeenth century but again in Chippendale period. See Reference No. CH1404.
Stretcher	The wooden connecting strut between legs of tables and chairs. See chair section for details of designs.
Stringing	Thin lines of inlay used as formal decoration, usually made in contrasting woods such as box, with possibly ebony and box patterning in later eighteenth century pieces. Used from early oak period – sixteenth century onwards.

Styles

The earliest decorative styles and designs on oak furniture of the late fifteenth and early sixteenth century, were influenced by the Gothic church architecture. It was not until the mix-sixteenth century that the Gothic influence was superseded by the Renaissance influence of continental designers and craftsmen, with the Germans and Flemish being the strongest.

During the seventeenth century the heavy bulbous furniture of Jacobean style was profusely carved and oak continued to be the predominant material until the last quarter of the century. However, Commonwealth furniture (1649 - 1660) introduced a lighter note, with barley-sugar twist and bobbin turning to legs and stretchers. The bulbous leg gave way to column turning with carved fluted decoration. Leather, held down by brass studs, began to be used as well as upholstery. With the restoration of the monarchy in 1660, a more extravagant note appeared in fashion and at last the decorative furniture associated with tasteful antique collecting began to appear. Walnut began to replace oak, slowly at first, but by 1680 walnut furniture, solid and veneered, was in general use. The arrival of many Huguenots after 1685 led to the further spread of decoratively veneered furniture, particularly marquetry, which, with walnut veneered furniture, was given further impetus by William III who brought in craftsmen from Holland where both styles were also popular. Furniture became more delicate in design, even if still very substantial by modern standards. In the Queen Anne period the cabriole leg became fashionable, having arrived from France and Italy via Holland.

It was during the first half of the eighteenth century that the architectural influence of designs became more evident on furniture styles. In particular William Kent, who was most influential between 1725 and 1740, showed the way to an overall conception of design covering the house and all its furnishings down to the smallest detail. Although most of his furniture was enormous, it reflected the design motifs of the time — broken pediments, eagles, festoons of fruit, ball-and-claw feet and so on. Mahogany made its appearance at this time and began generally to replace walnut furniture. The acanthus leaf was a popular motif and gilded furniture and japanning were also much in evidence.

From about 1740 the French rococo and Chinese tastes began to replace the heavier gilded ones and although Chippendale's famous book *'The Gentleman and Cabinet Makers Director'* was not published until 1754, it undoubtedly reflected previous and contemporary taste. Although it is now considered that little of the design work therein is original, and that much was copied from Lock and Copland's *'New Book of Ornaments'* published in 1746, it is nevertheless a very important work and the domestic furniture illustrated in it is now associated with the generic title of Chippendale Style. There were, in fact, three basic styles — Gothic, rococo and Chinese — which were the main source of material. Many of the pieces illustrated were not actually made and in later years the firm of Chippendale carried out work for and in the style of Robert Adam. The 'Chippendale' styles cover a period from c.1740 to c.1760.

After 1765 the style of Robert and James Adam became most influential. Like William Kent, Robert Adam believed in an overall concept of design covering house and all furnishings. He had studied a great deal in Italy and this style instigated the Classical Revival of which Syon House, Osterley and Kenwood are fine examples. It is in the second half of the eighteenth century that much of what is now considered to be the finest English furniture was produced under the influence of such designers as Adam and, of course, the published work of Chippendale, Shearer, Ince, and Mayhew, Batty Langley and Manwaring, while firms like Vile and Cobb, and Seddon, employed many craftsmen who spread the influences.

The Classical Revival instigated by Adam gradually superseded the Chinese, rococo and Gothic tastes. In 1788 George Hepplewhite's *'Cabinet Maker and Upholsterers Guide'* was published posthumously — he died in 1786 — and while his elegant and simple designs greatly influenced many cabinet makers, many of his motifs were similar to those of Adam. He is particularly associated with shield and oval back chairs and also the Prince of Wales' feathers as a motif. Thomas Sheraton, whose book *'The Cabinet Maker's and Upholsterer's Drawing Book'* was published in four parts starting in 1791, used many of the same motifs as Adam and Hepplewhite but his chairs were generally rectangular and he frequently used slim tapering square-section legs. He also favoured inlays and painting of furniture rather than carving legs for decoration.

In 1807 Thomas Hope published his book *'Household Furniture and Decoration'*. He had spent some years in Greece, Sicily and Egypt and was greatly influenced by Greek and Egyptian designs which became popular throughout the Regency period. Hope, like Sheraton, was not a cabinet maker, but George Smith, who also published in 1808 a book on furniture entitled *'A Collection of Designs for Household Furniture and Interior Decoration'*, was a practising craftsman. He also used Greek and Egyptian designs with Roman and Gothic styles as well. The Greek and Egyptian styles seem, however, to have been the more favoured of the period and by 1830 a rather formal, heavy approach was being used. Rosewood was popular as well as mahogany and machines had started to replace hand craftsmanship. This led to a lowering of the price of furniture and more pieces were crowded into the rooms of houses. After 1840 the classical styles began to give way to a revived form of Gothic and rococo, with rather heavy curves replacing the straight classical lines. The use of French Polish had commenced as well as the varnishing of pine pieces.

From about 1850 the furniture, now heavily crowded into every room, was a conglomerate of many styles, with rococo and Gothic still leading. Whether it was due to the overcrowding of pieces in each room, which led to over decoration in order to catch the eye, or from natural exuberance, is not clear, but decoration became excessive and many forms of carving and curved additions were superimposed on pieces which led to vulgarity. Perhaps some of the most pleasant pieces were those made in iron, which now came into use for garden furniture and chair and table legs.

The massive and overdecorated furniture continued to be produced up to the end of the nineteenth century, but in the last quarter of it some past designs became popular again. Chippendale, Sheraton and Hepplewhite styles were used, although in Victorianised form in many cases. Nevertheless, some very good reproductions of chairs were made at the end of the century. Otherwise the designs were over-embellished by the Victorians; the 'Sheraton' designs of the period, for instance, include much more inlay and a greater variety of woods than used originally. By the turn of the century nearly all designs were based on pre-1800 styles, even going back to Jacobean and Stuart. Although William Morris and later designers tried to produce original furniture based on medieval work in English woods, it was not altogether successful. In the Edwardian period the Art Nouveau movement produced some original work, but of doubtful endurance as an influence on furniture designs.

Sunburst A decoration of radiating lines or rays used particularly in the bottom drawers of tallboys and chests of the walnut period from 1700 to 1730. Made to look like the sun's rays and often inset in a concave shaping of the bottom drawer. See chest, Reference No. CH1421, and secretaire tallboy, B1511.

Swag A decorative form shaped like a hanging festoon, often made up of husks or flowers. Popular in the late eighteenth century on Adam and other furniture.

Swan-neck Term used to describe drop handles of eighteenth century form. See "Handles". Also used to describe the curve of a broken pediment cornice.

Tables See Sections.

Tallboy A chest upon a chest.

Tambour front A front made of strips of wood stuck side by side on canvas back to enable it to roll. A similar principle is used for a tambour shutter or sideboard and night tables. (NT1773).

Teapoy See Reference No. TP1810.

Tenon A joint form shaped to fix exactly into a cavity called a mortise. Used from the sixteenth century.

Tray-top A top of detachable type usually with a fretted opening in the vertical sides to act as a carrying handle. Also loosely used to describe the top of a night table, see Reference No. NT1772.

Veneer A thin sheet of wood which can be cut from the tree in several ways. The first real vogue for veneered furniture came in the walnut period 1680-1740 when the decorative effects of cutting veneers from walnut, laburnum, olive, tulipwood and so on, was appreciated. Originally these veneers were hand cut with a saw and were fairly thick — up to an eighth of an inch. They could be cut along the grain of the wood to give a straight, plain effect without much figure, or across the branches to form oysters (q.v.). Burr veneers were obtained by malformations of the grain due to injury, such as lopping.

Mahogany veneers of great decorative effect were also much used from about 1745, although the early Cuban mahogany was not much used for veneers. From the Victorian period paper thin veneers came into use and were obviously attractive because of the saving in wood. All modern veneered furniture is covered in these thin knife-cut sheets.

Wine Cooler See Reference No. CL1830.

WOODS

Amboyna A yellowish-brown burred surface somewhat between 'bird's-eye' maple and burr walnut. Used in the eighteenth century and on into the nineteenth, both for cross-banding and for whole surfaces. Origin: West Indies.

Apple One of the popular fruitwoods used in the solid for country pieces in the eighteenth century, although it had some use as a veneer earlier. A light reddish-brown in colour with some mild figuring. Fairly close-ground and hard, which gives a very satisfactory polish.

Ash A whitish-grey fairly hard wood used in country furniture in the eighteenth century and for drawer linings.

Beech A light brown surface with a distinctive flecked grain. Much loved by woodworm and used largely for chairs from the seventeenth century onwards. In the late Georgian and Regency periods it was painted, particularly in chair work. Early caned chairs of Restoration period were made from beech instead of walnut for economy and then ebonised.

Birch — A light yellowish-brown in colour and fairly soft. Used in eighteenth century for chairs and country furniture.

Boxwood — A whitish-yellow colour, without any figure. Used mainly as an inlay or for stringing lines from the sixteenth century.

Cedar — Reddish-brown, like a soft mahogany. Used for chests and interior work from the middle of the eighteenth century.

Cherry — Initially rather a pale wood but matures to a deeper reddish colour. Used for country furniture and for inlay or crossbanding from seventeenth century.

Chestnut — Horse chestnut is light, almost white and mainly found as a drawer lining material. Sweet chestnut matures to a reddish-brown and is reasonably hard for a country wood. Used for legs and in chairs from the seventeenth century.

Coromandel — A yellow and black striped wood used mainly for crossbanding from the late eighteenth century onwards.

Deal — Plain, straight-grained Scots pine. Used mainly for carcases (of chests, etc.) and drawer linings of lesser quality pieces. From seventeenth century onwards.

Ebony — Black, used for inlays.

Elm — Brown, with distinctive blackish figuring when old and ingrained with dirt. Another favourite of woodworms, and sometimes warps. Used extensively for country furniture and chairs, including seats of Windsors. Cut into burr veneers of fairly small sheets with extremely pleasing effect.

Harewood — This is just sycamore which has been stained to a greyish-green colour. Much used in later eighteenth century and Regency as a decorative veneer.

Holly	White, used for inlay and marquetry work from sixteenth century.
Kingwood	A brown and black striped wood like rosewood, particularly used for crossbanding on tables in late eighteenth century. Was used previously in late seventeenth century also as a veneer.
Laburnum	Cut as plain veneer, a yellow-brown with streaks of darker brown. Cut as an 'oyster' very dark rich blackish-brown. Used as veneer from late seventeenth century, particularly in parquetry.
Lignum vitae	Dark brown with black streaks. Very hard, used from seventeenth century as veneer and in solid.
Lime	Whitish-yellow; used by carvers.
Mahogany	Early mahogany, from 1720, was 'Spanish' or 'Cuban' from Cuba, Jamaica, San Domingo and Puerto Rico. Very dark, heavy with figuring. Later, 'Honduras' mahogany (originally called baywood) is lighter in colour and with a pinker tinge.
Maple	Light yellow; used as veneer and inlay. 'Bird's-eye' maple used more in the nineteenth century.
Oak	Early oak — before mid-seventeenth century — used in solid, has become usually very dark or plain brown colour. Later country oak furniture — of the eighteenth century — tends to be lighter and the distinctive 'wormlike' yellow rays are more visible. In fine furniture of late seventeenth and eighteenth centuries, oak was used for drawer linings in plain sawn form, and especially in inner drawers remains light in colour. Also used in veneer form.
Olive	Dark, greenish with black streaking. Used in parquetry, as 'oyster' and in veneers, from late seventeenth century.
Padouk	Red, with blackish figure. Used in solid from mid-eighteenth century and particularly from early nineteenth for military chests.

Pear	Yellowish-brown. Used for country furniture and for carving.
Pine	See "Deal".
Plum	Yellowish-red. Used for country pieces and as an inlay from the seventeenth century.
Rosewood	Usually reddish-brown with black streaks, but fades to a greyer colour, still with dark streaks. Used from the sixteenth century but mostly found in Regency period in solid and veneer.
Satinwood	Yellow. Used particularly from the late eighteenth century in veneer and solid. Usually makes for price premium.
Sycamore	White with fleck. Used from the late seventeenth century as a veneer. Often found on sides or banding of marquetry furniture of the late seventeenth or early eighteenth century.
Tulipwood	Yellow-brown with reddish stripes. Used for crossbanding from the late eighteenth century.
Walnut	English walnut: golden brown with dark figuring. Very decoratively used in veneers from the sixteenth century but particularly 1660-1740. Also cut in burr and oyster form. Solid walnut used extensively in Tudor period and later for chairs, stands and country pieces.
	Black walnut: also grown in England from the late seventeenth century; usually called 'Virginian' walnut and much darker. Used in solid and can be mistaken for mahogany at first glance.
Yew	Reddish-brown, very hard, with some burr effects. Polishes mangificently. Used from the sixteenth century; often found in chairs of country origin. Windsors and tables but also used on fine furniture in burr veneer form. Beloved by fakers since it is easier to 'age' in appearance. Many estate-made and Victorian pieces used it.
Zebra-wood	Brown with dark stripes. Used as a veneer from the late eighteenth century.

CHAIRS

In the 200-year period covered by this section the number of designs of chairs which emerged was almost infinite. In fact, of all the antique pieces of furniture under review, the chair is the one most difficult to illustrate comprehensively. Nevertheless, the ninety or so examples in this section show the main generic types.

Apart from the value points mentioned under individual items, the following points relate particularly to chairs and must be taken to be common to all of them:-

1. Structural condition and originality. Chairs in particular are subject to high stresses in use; their structural condition is highly important. Many chairs had stretchers replaced due to this, but on early chairs this does not affect value as much as other replacements. What is important is to ascertain whether any legs or uprights have been replaced. Splats are also particularly subject to breakage and replacement. The joints between top rail and uprights on the back are often damaged and repaired. The combination of good structural condition and originality are therefore to be regarded as a +++ factor and possibly a ++++ factor in chairs before 1740.

2. Colour and patination. Good colour — particularly a little fading in walnut examples — and the patination of surface caused by polishing over the years, provide a ++ factor in chair values. Patination in chairs is not quite so important as it is with pieces of furniture with larger surface areas, but nevertheless values are affected accordingly.

3. Original upholstery. In chairs affected by this factor, the possession of original upholstery and covering fabrics undoubtedly provides a +++ factor at least.

4. In chairs with cabriole legs, we have referred to the quality of them. To define this requires an appreciation almost impossible to set down in print; the design and execution of cabriole legs demands great craftsmanship to be successful. A cabriole leg can be bold and graceful with success; the imperative requirement is that it should not lose proportion or relation to the rest of the chair.

5. Sets of chairs. The value of a chair increases rapidly when it is part of a set, but not proportionately. A single chair may be desirable for its particular design or quality as a decorative piece and a pair of chairs are usually regarded as a greater asset as far as individual price is concerned. A set of three chairs, however, is regarded by many dealers as something of a bête noir, and they are often separated into a single and a pair for purposes of sale. A set of four chairs comes into a much better value-per-chair range but this is rightly regarded as a very small set in terms of use for family or entertainment of guests. Six chairs in a set, however, are desirable goods in practically any style and cause a sharp rise in individual chair value. A set of more than six chairs continues this trend.

ref. **C1000 (3)**

Mid-seventeenth century chair in oak, with elaborately carved back, c.1650.

The earlier seventeenth century forms of chair were not dissimilar from this, with the exception of the elaborate winged scrolls on the uprights. Earlier chairs tended to be simpler, with square backs and the decorative areas were less profusely carved. Later in the century the carving exhibited a variety of motives. Note the heavy construction, with column turned legs and square stretchers. Simpler chairs have 'scratchings' in diamond or other shapes in place of the carvings. Large quantities of these chairs were made, often with dates and initials of owners. Some are decorated with inlays of box, holly (white), and ebony (black) in geometrical and floral designs. Country makers continued to produce them until the early eighteenth century.

Price Range: Very wide and geared to quality of inlay and carving. Prices of £100 – £150 relate to highly carved versions; simple ones with scratch decoration are to be found at £30 – £50.

Value points therefore: Quality of carving +++

Warning: Victorian 'improvers' tended to add initials, dates and carving to simple chairs.

ref. **C1001 (4)**

Mid-seventeenth century chair in oak, c.1650. Note the diamond-shaped scratch decoration in the panelled back and solid pegged seat. The front legs are turned in rather bulbous baluster fashion, but the joints remain square, and the pegs in the floor-level square section stretcher tenon joints can be seen. The seat is very worn but the remains of the moulded edge can be seen along the rear left-hand side. The front rail is carved in the same decorative manner as the back and shaped on the lower edge; again the pegged tenon joints are evident.

Price Range: *Not at present a popular taste. Single chair £35 – £45.*

Value points: Quality of turning and carving +++

ref. **C1002(5)**

A mid-seventeenth century country oak chair, c.1650, of pleasing simplicity and robust construction. The legs are still column turned as in our previous example and left square at the joints for the tenons, which were pegged. The back is panelled and without decoration. Not a popular collector's chair at present but still well within reach of the modest pocket.

Price Range: £30 – £40

Value points: *Quality of turning and decoration if any +++*

ref. **C1003 (6)**

An oak 'Derbyshire chair' of c.1650, showing the arcaded back and split baluster decoration on the uprights. Note that the seat is inset or dished to allow for a cushion.

Price Range: £30 – £40

Value points: Quality of carving and turning +++

N.B. The chair in the illustration is a reproduction.

ref. **C1004 (7)**

Cromwellian chair, c.1660, demonstrating movement towards lighter design still based on turning. The twist turning was popular in the period and the piece is made of walnut, a wood much more commonly used in the seventeenth century than is generally supposed. The chair is covered with leather fixed to the frame with heavy nails. Not a chair commonly found in antique shops; it is of a specialist collector's taste. Bobbin turning rather than twist is often found and beech as well as oak or walnut was used.

Price Range: Single chair £40 – £50
                 Sets £80 – £100
Value points: Walnut +++
                 Oak +
                 Twist turning +++

ref. **C1005 (8)**

Cromwellian oak chair, c.1660, of country construction. Note the square outline and the retention of the floor level square stretchers. The back is straight and the turning simple.

Price Range: Single: £25 – £35
               Sets: £50 – £60

ref. **C1006 (9)**
A Charles II – c.1675 – oak chair of radical development. The design is of Continental influence and more continuous. Apart from being carved the design of the scroll both on legs, front stretcher and back, serves to obscure rather than emphasize the method of construction. Cane backs were introduced around 1665 and help to lighten the overall appearance. Twist turning is still evident as well as the square back leg and stretcher joints.
Price Range: Single £60 – £80
Value points: Carving, particularly of front stretcher which can be very ornate +++
                Walnut +++

ref. **C1007 (10)**
Simple oak chair of Charles II period, c.1675, with cane back. The front stretcher is simply turned and the seat has been upholstered, perhaps later. The quality is indicated by the fine sweep of the arms and the execution of the carved top cresting rail.

Price Range: £80 – £100
Value points: Carving +++

ref. **C1008 (11)**

An oak armchair of c.1680. Note that the stretchers also exhibit twist turning as well as all the uprights. The back carving is well executed with the top rail and front stretcher showing two cherubs supporting a coronet — 'boyes and crownes'. These chairs, taken singly, are still somewhat undervalued although sets are a specialist demand and command high prices. The back and seat were probably caned originally.

Price Range: £60 – £70

Value points: *Quality of carving +++*
                  Walnut +++

ref. **C1009 (13)**
Late seventeenth century country walnut chair, c.1680. Note the high back. Rather than incur the expense of the cane back of the town example the country craftsmen used vertical solid bars. The stretchers still follow earlier designs with simple turning and square sections at the tenon joints. The uprights are turned.

Price Range: Single £35 – £45

ref. **C1010 (14)**
Three more late seventeenth century country chairs - c.1690 in oak, showing the variations possible in the back. The squab seats have been added for comfort. It is interesting not only to see the similarity of leg and stretcher construction but the variations possible in the turning of them.

Price Range: Single £30 – £40
              Pair   £70 – £90

Value points: Quality of execution and carving of back +++
              Walnut +++

ref. **C1011 (15)**

A late seventeenth century chair of c.1695 in walnut, with velvet upholstery. The cross stretcher was a feature of the decade 1685 - 1695 and in this case it is moulded. The carved legs show a development of the inverted cup form of Dutch origin: here it is scrolled and the square joints of these front legs are also decorated. This scrolling was of French stylistic influence.

Price Range: *£150 – £200*

Value points: Quality of leg and stretcher carving +++
Original upholstery +++

ref. **C1012 (16)**

Late seventeenth century — William and Mary period — walnut armchair, c.1695. Curved and moulded stretchers. Note the bulb turning and 'bun' feet — to be seen on other pieces of the period such as side tables and chest stands. The wool or hair upholstery is covered with velvet with bullion braiding. Note also the curvature of the arms to balance the stretchers.

Price Range: £120 – £150 *for this quality. Chairs of this period tend to be uncommon and wide variations occur depending on condition and quality.*

Value points: *Walnut +++*
Balancing of design of arms and stretchers +++
Quality of turning ++

ref. **C1013 (17)**

William and Mary period walnut chair c.1700 with cane back. A marked development in design from the previous example. The high cane back and square section joining of the back legs has been retained but the new form of leg – the cabriole – has appeared, introduced to England by foreign workmen. The cabrioles in this example finish in hoof or pied-de-biche feet. This is an early form of Continental influence. The transition between the high backed cane chairs of the seventeenth century and the finely carved cabrioles of the eighteenth century is to be seen. The Victorians were fond of making hall chairs of this type but usually lost proportion in legs and stretchers.

Price Range: Single *£200 – £250*

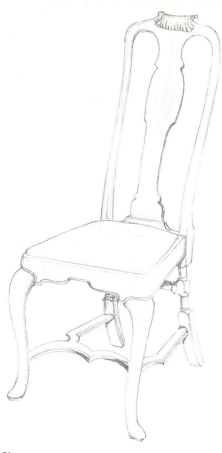

ref. **C1014 (18)**
Queen Anne period walnut chair c.1710 of early design. The now famous splat shape is evident but the high back is retained, although a curve in the rake of the back has emerged — the spoon back. There is a shaped and moulded stretcher but in this case the cabriole legs terminate in simple pad feet. The height of the back and the square section of the back legs are retained from the previous century. An interesting feature peculiar to Q. A. workmanship is the slightly raised planed moulding at the bottom of the frame just under the seat, rather like cockbeading. Cabriole-leg side tables and chest stands of the period sometimes exhibit the same feature.

Price Range: *Single £90 – £110*
                Pair   *£250 – £300*

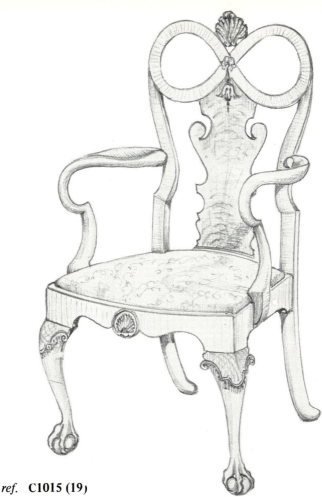

ref. **C1015 (19)**

A superb walnut armchair of about 1720 raised on high quality cabriole legs decorated on the knee with criss cross carving and small tassels, the ends terminating in ball and claw feet. The back is of unusual shape but the solid splat of walnut veneered on oak is found on less good examples. The shepherd's crook arms are well proportioned. The thick rim round the drop-in seat is typical of the period, as is the shell motif repeated on the cresting rail. A side view would show the pronounced rake of this top quality chair.

Price Range: *£500 – £700*
Value points: *Cabrioles +++*
                  Back +++
                  Arms +++

ref. **C1016 (20)**

A Queen Anne period country walnut chair, c.1710, which was originally rush-seated. The front legs are cabrioles and the turned stretchers between the legs have square joints. The presence of stretchers tends to distract somewhat from the line of the cabrioles and is generally assumed to be a feature of the chairs of the earlier part of the period. The back legs and uprights are also turned, a feature frequently found on chairs of this period. The plain back splat is curved and the rush seat was of the drop-in type. The cabriole legs end in pad feet and the design and execution of the chair is of good quality for country furniture. Instead of fitting shoulder pieces at the sides of the cabriole knees, the flat facets are covered with round knobs, glued on.

Price Range: Single £40 – £50   Pair £80 – £110
                  Four £250 – £400   Six £500 – £700

Value points: *Quality of cabriole and back* ++
                  Note the cabrioles on this example are slightly bandy and the knee (top) is too heavy for the foot.

ref. **C1017**

An oak Queen Anne period country chair, c.1710. The back splat is of the shape typically associated with the period. The termination of the uprights is very interesting because the line has been carried into the top rail and over to a pointed termination where the splat joins it. The front rail is rather heavy, but shaped, and the cabriole legs are gently curved, ending in simple pad feet. The rather rigid back legs and lack of rake emphasize the country origin. The solid seat has a typical shallow moulding around it, probably originally fitted to retain a squab cushion.

Price Range:		Walnut	Oak
	Single	£50 – £60	£25 – £35
	Pair	£120 – £140	£60 – £90
	Four	£250 – £400	£160 – £200
	Six	£500 – £700	£300+

Value points: *Colour and quality of design +++*
Original stretchers +

ref. **C1018 (22)**

Walnut Queen Anne period corner chair with inlaid diamond pattern in boxwood. Turned stretchers and uprights. Typically shaped splats in figured walnut. Drop-in seat. Cabriole legs ending in pad feet; note the shell motif carved on the front cabriole, a + factor of quality. This chair is possibly of country origin.

Price Range: £100 – £150. *Generally a man's taste.*

Value points: Quality of execution, i.e. proportion, grace of cabrioles, shell motifs etc. +++
All legs cabrioles +++ (sometimes the back and side legs are left straight or turned, detracting from value).

ref. **C1019 (24)**

A George II period mahogany chair, c.1735. Note that although a fine quality Cuban mahogany has been used, the style is one which would normally be associated with walnut; but there are extra refinements. The vase shaped splat has small scrolls and a shell work top. The shaped uprights to the back are topped with eagle heads and the cabriole legs have leaf patterns carved on the knees.

Price Range: *Single chair £90 – £110*
               In sets   *£175 – £230 per chair*
Value points: *Quality of carving +++*

ref. **C1020 (26)**

Walnut pre-Chippendale chair of c.1740 - 50. Cabriole legs with scroll and leaf on knee, ending in pad feet. Top rail and upright meet in elegant scroll. Pierced splat designed to give four tapering uprights. Drop-in seat. A chair of some quality even if possibly provincially made.

Price Range:	Single	£35 – £45	
	Pair	£90 – £110	
	Four	£190 – £225	
	Six	£400 – £600	
Value points:	Proportion ++		
	Note the outward sweep of back legs, terminating in knobs to balance front pad feet.		

ref. **C1021 (27)**

Another walnut pre-Chippendale chair with simpler but similar back splat design. The square legs and stretchers suggest a later date — possibly 1750 — and the proportions are a little less ample, but this is nevertheless a very pleasing chair. There is a drop-in seat and the front legs have a scratch moulding down the front corners; they are chamfered at the back.

Price Range: Single   £15 – £25
                  Pair   £45 – £60
                  Four   £100 – £150
                  Six   £150 – £250

Value points: Proportion ++
                   Quality and execution of back splats +++

ref. **C1022 (28)**

An interesting chair of c.1755 in mahogany, the kneed legs showing the provincial type transition to square straight legs from cabrioles. The scrolled carving of the splat is elegantly done yet the chair retains the essential sturdiness of the period. The proportion is good and the back legs sweep boldly back in the manner of earlier chairs.

Price Range: Single   £25 – £30
*   Pair   £70 – £90*
*   Four   £250 – £350*
*   Six   £450 – £750*
Value points: Balance and proportion +++
*   Quality of splat carving +++*

ref. **C1023 (29)**

Chippendale mahogany armchair of considerable quality, c.1760. Cabriole legs, decorated with shell and scroll pattern carving on the knee, terminating in excellent ball-and-claw feet. The arms sweep boldly outwards, terminating almost at right angles to the line of the sides in scrolls. A very well proportioned back splat, with the upper scrolled curves leading perfectly from the top rail, which is also carved with leaf patterns. Note the boldness and width of the fully upholstered seat which is covered in leather. N.B. Although this type is generally known as a 'Chippendale' chair, it is interesting to recall that the *'Director'* shows chairs with cabriole legs with scrolled feet, until the third edition, when a plate of hall chairs shows the ball and claw foot, which was undoubtedly popular at this period.

Price Range: £300 – £400

Value points: Quality and execution of cabrioles +++
Quality of back splat and carving +++

Warning: Many high quality Victorian reproductions exist of this type of chair. These reproductions have a value of £25 – £35 each.

ref. **C1024(30)**

Chippendale mahogany armchair, c.1760, again of considerable quality, particularly in the carving of the centre splat and top rail. The straight front legs are reeded, as are the curving uprights. There is less sweep to the arms and the plainer treatment of the legs reduces the value from the previous example. The boldness and width of the chair are particularly to be noted in that nineteenth century copies tend to be meaner in proportion. The craftsmanship in the carving of the back splat is of a high order.

Price Range: £200 – £275

Value points: Quality and execution of carving +++
Proportion ++

ref. **C1025 (31)**

A single mahogany Chippendale chair, c.1760, of similar type to the preceding armchair but of bolder proportion. While the back uprights are reeded however, the legs are not. A scratch moulding down the corners of the front legs gives added lightness and the front apron is slightly serpentine. Note the very fine quality of the scroll and leaf carving which is pleasantly mellowed with age and lacks the sharpness of a reproduction piece. The overall proportions of the chair are extremely pleasing and demonstrate the ample size of eighteenth century seats.

Price Range: *Single*   *£75 –   £100*
                Pair   *£150 – £200*
                Four   *£400 – £700*
                Six   *£750 – £1,500*

Value points: *Proportion +++*
                Quality of carving +++

ref. **C1026 (32)**

Chippendale mahogany chair in the Gothic style, c.1755. Although the Gothic influence – and French influence also – are evident, it is only in mild form in this chair. In earlier versions taken from Chippendale's *'Director'* the Gothic designs are very much more exaggerated, with multi-arched backs and heavily fretted legs and stretchers. This chair is of high quality, good proportion and restrained, though righ, execution. (Gothic and Chinese Chippendale chairs of high quality are much sought-after).

Price Range:	Single	£100 – £130
	Pair	£250 – £300
	Four	£600 – £800
	Six	£1,000 upwards.

Value points: Quality and design, proportion and carving +++

ref. **C1027 (33)**

A mahogany Chippendale chair, c.1760, with the splat again showing the Gothic influence in the arching. The top rail is waved and carved with leaves, but the legs and stretchers are the plain robust design of the period.

Price Range: *Single*   *£80 – £100*
                    Pair   *£175 – £250*
                    Four   *£400 – £600*
                    Six   *£750 – £1,000*

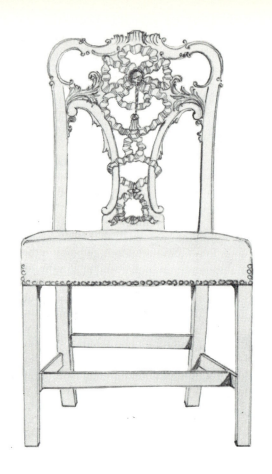

ref. **C1028 (34)**

A Chippendale 'Ribbon' back chair of c.1760 - 70. So called because of the ribbon carving in the back. Due to the craftsmanship involved in executing these chairs they naturally command high prices and are relatively scarce. The remainder of the chair is of typical Chippendale design, with fully upholstered seat which in some cases may be serpentine at the front. It is interesting to note that although the period after 1730 - 40 is generally associated with mahogany, a well known example of this type exists in walnut, and walnut chairs are to be found of even later date.

Price Range: Single £125 – £175

Value points: As for previous Chippendale chairs.

ref. **C1029 (35)**

Country Chippendale armchair in elm c.1770. A simple and appeallingly bold chair although this example has been worn or slightly cut down in the leg. The seat is fully upholstered, which may be a conversion due to damage to the front rail. The tenon joints are pegged.

Price Range: £30 – £40

Value points: Colour, figure and patination ++
Quality of splat ++

ref. **C1030 (36)**

Another Country Chippendale armchair — c.1770 — of more ornate splat design, with drop-in seat. The Gothic influence is evident in the arching within the splat and the top rail is also arched in a slightly later style. Usually to be found in mahogany or country wood such as elm or birch stained mahogany colour.

Price Range: *Mahogany*   £45 – £55
               Country Wood £35 – £45

Value points: Quality of splat carving ++

Warning: Many such chairs, having been used hard for many years, have had stretchers replaced or cut legs replaced. Watch also for broken or replaced splats and top rails; the latter particularly at the tenon joint with the upright.

ref. **C1031 (37)**

A Chippendale mahogany ladder-back chair of c.1765. The ladder-back designs tended to be of later Chippendale period. In this case the back rails are elegantly designed and pieced to add lightness to the overall effect. Note the scratch moulding down the front leg corners also to add lightness and the chamfered backs of the front legs.

Price Range: Single   £50 – £60
                    Pair   £100 – £120
                    Four   £250 – £350
                    Six   £400 – £600

Value points: *Quality and carving of ladder rails +++*
                    Proportion ++

ref. **C1032 (38)**

A Chippendale ladder-back chair — c.1770 — with upholstered seat, slightly shaped across the front rail. The pierced rails of the ladder-back help to lighten the chair.

Price Range: Single   £40 – £50
 Pair   £100 – £120
 Four   £180 – £250
 Six   £400 – £500

ref. **C1033 (39)**
Country Chippendale chair in mahogany c.1760. Fully upholstered seat covered in tapestry pattern fabric. A good example of a better quality country chair.

Price Range: Single   £20 – £30
      Pair   £40 – £60
      Four   £90 – £120
      Six   £250 – £350

ref. **C1034 (40)**

Country Chippendale chair in birch, originally stained to look like mahogany. Rather later in date – last quarter of the eighteenth century – c.1785 – with considerable Gothic influence in the carving of the splat. Less bold in execution than the earlier chairs but nevertheless a pleasant country chair frequently collected in odd numbers to make up 'harlequin' sets i.e. sets of similar style but not matching designs.

Price Range: Single   £10   –   £20-
               Pair   £20   –   £40
               Four   £60   –   £90
               Six   £120   –   £200

ref. **C1035 (41)**
Mahogany Chippendale chair of pleasing simplicity and proportion, c.1780. The splat is elegantly curved and the back, though square in design, is curved and softened by the tapering uprights.

Price Range:	Single	£20 – £30
	Pair	£40 – £60
	Four	£100 – £150
	Six	£200 – £300

Value points: Proportion and quality of workmanship +++

ref. **C1036 (42)**

Plain Country Chippendale chair with solid seat. To be found in mahogany, oak, elm, birch, fruitwood and sometimes even walnut. Made in the country from 1760 onwards, probably to end of century at least.

Price Range:		Oak, Elm, Birch etc.	Walnut & Fruitwood
	Single	£10 – £15	£15 – £25
	Pair	£20 – £40	£40 – £60
	Four	£60 – £80	£80 – £120
	Six	£100 – £150	£150 – £200

ref. **C1037 (43)**

An oak country chair of c.1760 with solid seat. The back splat still retains an echo of the Queen Anne period but the uprights and top rail join in an outward turn more akin the mid-eighteenth century. Similar chairs in solid walnut with even earlier styles in the back pre-date these simple robust pieces.

Price Range:	Single chair	£15 – £20
	In sets	£25 – £35

ref. **C1038 (44)**

A mahogany Chippendale chair with fully upholstered seat, c.1770. The back splat design is one which seems to have been particularly popular with country and later makers of this design of chair.

Price Range: *Single*   £25 –   £30
                Pair   £60 –   £80
                Four   £120 – £160
                Six   £220 – £280

ref. **C1039 (45)**

Mahogany Country Chippendale chair of heavier proportion c.1780. The casters under the legs have been added later, possibly to compensate for wear caused by stone floors. There is considerable workmanship in the carving of the back but the rather flattened top rail lacks the elegance of London or even provincial work.

Price Range: *Single*   *£20 – £25*
                 Pair   *£50 – £60*
                 Four   *£100 – £150*
                 Six   *£180 – £250*

Value points: *As for other Chippendale chairs.*

ref. **C1040 (46)**

A 'Chipplewhite' design mahogany chair of c.1780. Note that the influence of French designs has now cut the bold sweep of the arms to a more attenuated length and of less broad a scope.

Price Range: £40 – £60
Value points: Quality of back and splat +++

ref. **C1041 (47)**
Hepplewhite chairs of hooped back design, c.1790. The tapering legs are reeded or moulded and the back repeats this feature. Note that the armchair is not a match with the single chairs. The back splat designs are typical of this type, finely executed and decorated with carving down the centre.

Price Range:	Single chair	£40 – £50	Set of 2 arm, 4 singles	£600 – £750
	Arm	£50 – £70	Set of 2 arm, 6 singles	£1,000 +

ref. **C1042 (48)**

A Hepplewhite design chair of c.1790 with hooped back. The centre splat decorated with the circular medal-like motif with leaf decoration radiating out from a centre. A fairly typical design which is associated with Hepplewhite but which more probably emanated from Robert Adam. The legs are still of the square section straight type of Chippendale period and not as light or elegant as the normal Hepplewhite type which were tapered. The seat is bowed. The chair is made of mahogany.

Price Range: *Single* £40 – £60
Pair £90 – £120
Four £250 – £350
Six £450 – £600

ref. **C1043 (49)**

Fine quality Hepplewhite arm and single chair, c.1790. Note the leaf carving on the back and round the top rail to finish half way down the uprights. The influence of Robert Adam is evident in these.

Price Range:	Single chair	£30 – £50
	Arm	£60 – £90
	Set of 2 arm and 4 single	£650 – £750
	Set of 2 arm and 6 single	£1,000 +

ref. **C1044 (50)**
A mahogany Hepplewhite chair of pleasing proportions, c.1790. The arms show the more restrained curves of the late eighteenth century although the seat, legs and stretchers are still bold and firm in proportion.

Price Range: £45 – £60

Value points: Quality of back splat carving +++

ref. **C1045 (51)**

A mahogany Hepplewhite chair – c.1790 – which suggests a development from a Chippendale design rather than a break from it. The structure is very similar; the front legs are not tapered on the inside edge and the camel-back form of top back rail tempers the outward sweep of the uprights.

Price Range: Single £30 – £50
　　　　　　　Pair　　£60 – £100
　　　　　　　Four　　£150 – £300
　　　　　　　Six　　　£350 – £500

Value points: This is a simple version of this design. A more decorated version could well double these prices.

ref. **C1046 (52)**

A Country Hepplewhite design chair, c.1795, of a type most frequently found made in elm. Normally they are stained or varnished to look like mahogany, and have been stripped and polished later if now in the natural wood. The design is known as a camel-back and is a logical development of the town-made mahogany one; simpler in execution and less decorated.

Price Range: Single £10 – £15
Pair £25 – £40
Four £50 – £80
Six £100 – £150

Value points: Proportion and design +++

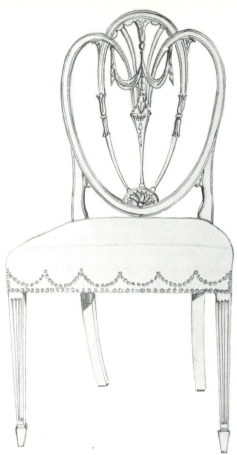

ref. **C1048 (53)**

Hepplewhite shield-back chair c.1790. The carving of the back is of particularly fine quality. The tapering legs are fluted and the decoration of brass studs adds further ornamentation. Normally executed in mahogany. Front legs end in spade feet.

Price Range: *Considered by many to be a high point in English design, original shield back Hepplewhite chairs fetch very high prices. Those below are an indication:-*

                        Single   *£100 – £120*
                        Pair   *£350 – £400*
                        Four   *£800 – £1,000*
                        Six   *£1,200 – £1,500*

Value points: *Quality of carving and motifs +++*
                    Proportion and design +++

ref. **C1047 (54)**

Hepplewhite mahogany shield-back arm and single chair c.1790. The craftsmanship involved in making a successful shield-back chair is of the highest order and to obtain the necessary degree of comfort and stability as well as fine proportion is a task of considerable difficulty. The central balusters of these two fine chairs are joined to the top rail by the 'Prince of Wales feathers', a very favourite motif with Hepplewhite and one which was emphasized in his Guide. The shield-backs are edged with a small double beading on the inner and outer edges. The legs on these are not reeded and there is less decoration than that of the preceding example; the front legs end in spade feet.

Price Range:	Single	£80 – £100
	Arm	£100 – £150
	Pair	£200 – £220
	Four	£400 – £500
	Six	£600 – £900

Value points: *Proportion and quality of carving +++*
Structural condition and originality +++

ref. **C1049 (55)**

A mahogany chair of c.1790 of a design also associated with Hepplewhite although some of the conflicting trends of eighteenth century designs are evident in the square legs and eight pointed wheel effect. It is a fairly simple version of a beautiful design and represents a considerable accomplishment in craftsmanship. Note that the front legs end in spade feet.

Price Range: £250 – £300

Value points: Quality and execution of back +++

ref. **C1050 (56)**

A Sheraton design chair of considerable workmanship, c.1795. Many such chairs are to be found painted in white and gilt or otherwise having painted decoration on birch or beech wood. In the main the painted versions are more highly sought after than the mahogany ones, which makes for higher prices. Note the turned and fluted legs. The arm uprights have spiral reeding.

Price Range: *£200 – £250*

ref. **C1051 (57)**

A later Georgian chair of Sheraton influence, c.1800, in the back but with arms more associated with Hepplewhite styles. The tapering front legs and the back are moulded; a mark of quality.

Price Range: £40 – £60

ref. **C1052 (58)**

A Sheraton design arm and single chair in mahogany, c.1795. The uprights and arms are reeded, which lightens the square solidity of design. Note the vase shaped turned arm supports and the way in which the broad top rail is panelled.

Price Range: *Single £20 – £25*
                         Arm £45 – £60
                         Set of 2 arm and 4 single £250 – £300
                         Set of 2 arm and 6 single £400 – £600

ref. **C1053 (59)**

A country version of the two previous Sheraton style chairs, c.1810. The seats are solid and the back leg and upright very much straighter and rigid, with very little rake. The backs are also simplified; the front stretcher is placed high between the two front legs as with earlier chairs instead of between the two side stretchers.

Price Range: Single   £10 – £15
                      Arm   £20 – £30
                      Set of 2 arm and 4 single £100 – £150
                      Set of 2 arm and 6 single £175 – £250

ref. **C1054 (60)**

A Sheraton style arm and single chair in mahogany, c.1800. The legs and back uprights are reeded; this effect is also carried round the panel in the wider top back rail.

Price Range: Single   £25 – £35
                     Arm   £40 – £50
                     2 arm and 4 single £300 – £400
                     2 arm and 6 single £500 – £700

ref. **C1055 (61)**
A simpler Sheraton design with tapering legs normally made in mahogany, c.1800. The arm uprights are of straightforward turning without the spiral reeding which adds greatly to price. An elegant and simple style which remained popular for many years.

Price Range: *Single armchair £60 – £80*
Value points: *Quality and proportion of design +++*

ref. **C1056 (62)**

A mahogany Sheraton style single chair, c.1800, with Gothic arching in the design of the back. The legs are tapered on the inside edge only and are reeded, as is the back. An elegant and simple chair.

Price Range:	Single	£30 – £40
	Pair	£60 – £90
	Four	£150 – £250
	Six	£300 – £500

ref. **C1057 (63)**

Late eighteenth century arm and single chairs, c.1800. Note the broad top rail in the back, the panel veneered in figured mahogany. The spiral twist middle rail is a feature of quality particularly important in value assessment of these chairs. The legs are turned, without any fluting. The arms of the elbow chair sweep forward and curve down to meet the line of the front legs. The proportion of these admirable smaller dining chairs makes them extremely popular in the modern home.

Price Range:	Armchair	£30 – £50
	Pair armchairs	£80 – £100
	Single chair	£20 – £25
	Pair	£40 – £50
	Four	£100 – £150
	Six	£200 – £300

ref. **C1058 (64)**

A mahogany armchair of c.1800 date. An excellent example of a good quality chair, as evidenced in the reeding and lightness of design of the back. The turned legs are a little clumsier and have hints of later things to come.

Price Range: £50 – £70

Value points: *Quality and proportion of overall design +++*
                           Quality of carving and turning +++

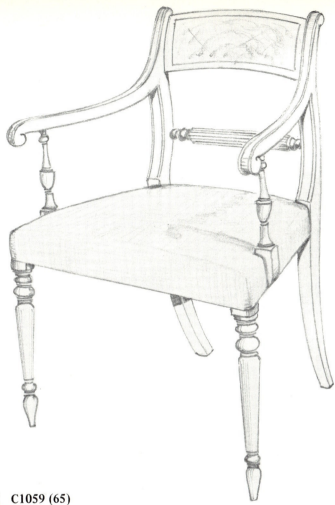

ref. C1059 (65)

Another late Georgian c.1810 mahogany armchair, something of a combination of Sheraton and prevailing styles. The wide top back rail is veneered with a panel of figured mahogany and the centre rail is elegantly reeded. The turning of the front legs and the arm supports, with the popular vase shape, is lightly and gracefully done. Occasionally brass stringing will be found around the inlaid back panel, which adds to the decorative value.

Price Range: £35 – £50

Value points: *Proportion and design +++*
Figure of wood and inlays +++

ref. **C1060 (66)**

Country Sheraton design armchair in mahogany with bowed solid seat, c.1810. A satisfying and simple country design of which many were made to meet the popular demand caused by the town versions.

Price Range: *£20 – £30*
Value points: *As for town Sheraton chairs.*

ref. **C1061 (67)**

A country Sheraton single chair in mahogany with straight legs and solid seat, c.1810. The square back with vertical rails owes much to the popularity of Sheraton styles, otherwise the design comes from a straightforward eighteenth century construction.

Price Range:	Single	£10 – £12
	Pair	£20 – £25
	Four	£50 – £60
	Six	£90 – £120

ref. **C1062 (68)**

A very simplified country chair of c.1800. The design owes something to Sheraton in the tapering front legs and squared style of the back. The two horizontal rails are very plain and more ornamented versions are to be found. The solid bowed seat is made of elm and the rest of the chair is fruitwood.

Price Range:	Single	£5 – £10
	Pair	£12 – £20
	Four	£30 – £50
	Six	£60 – £90

ref. **1063 (69)**

A rather heavier Sheraton style mahogany country chair with drop-in seat, c.1810. The broad top rail of the back has been made slightly wider than the back uprights which detracts slightly from the elegance of the style. Otherwise the construction and tapering legs are typical.

Price Range:	Single	£12 – £15
	Pair	£25 – £30
	Four	£60 – £70
	Six	£100 – £150

ref. **1064 (70)**

Late eighteenth/early nineteenth century oak spindle-back chairs, sometimes called 'Lancashire' chairs. They are rush-seated and are sometimes made of elm.

Price Range: *Single chair*   *£10 – £15*
                 Arm   *£20 – £25*
                 Six   *£100 – £150*

ref. **C1065 (71)**

An elegant chair of the early Regency period, c.1820, with caned back and seat. The outward turn of the simulated bamboo legs is most effective and the balance is completed by the curved top rail. The seat rail and the top rail are inlaid with stringing in the approved classical manner. Many of these chairs were made of birch or beech and then ebonised or painted. They are almost inevitably very expensive.

Price Range:	Single Arm	£80 –	£90
	Pair	£180 –	£250
	Four	£450 –	£500
	Six	£750 –	£1,000

Value points: *Lightness and elegance of design +++*
　　　　　　　 Decoration +++

ref. **C1066 (72)**

Another very elegant Regency chair, c.1825, with rope twist motif on the back and sabre legs. The caned seat again adds to the overall lightness of design.

Price Range:	Single	£50 –	£60
	Pair	£100 –	£120
	Four	£250 –	£400
	Six	£750 –	£1,000

ref. **C1067 (73)**

A Regency arm and single chair, c.1825, similar to the previous example in rope twist design but with drop in seats instead of cane. The panel between the horizontal rails in the back is inlaid with brass.

Price Range: *Single chair £45 – £55*
                     Arm   *£60 – £80*
                     Set of 2 arm and 4 single £500 – £750
                     Set of 2 arm and 6 single £750 +

ref. **C1068 (74)**

A mahogany Regency chair with lyre motif in the back, c.1825. The curved side rails and sabre legs are reeded to give a continuous effect. The drop-in seat is located by a peg set in the top of the front rail. As with all sabre-leg chairs the front legs should be examined carefully to see whether the top has been damaged; the construction of a sabre leg necessitates cutting across the grain of the wood thereby reducing the strength of the timber. It is a sign of quality if there are none of these repairs.

Price Range:	Single	£45 – £65
	Pair	£100 – £150
	Four	£200 – £300
	Six	£500 – £750

For some reason the lyre causes a rush of blood to the head in chair purchasers; look for inflated values accordingly.

ref. **C1069 (75)**

A similar pair of Regency chairs with reeding continuous down back uprights, sides and sabre legs. The carved decoration is simple and elegant, c.1830

Price Range:	Single	£20 – £30
	Pair	£50 – £60
	Four	£150 – £200
	Six	£250 – £350

ref. **C1070 (76)**

A typical Regency mahogany sabre-leg chair of pleasing proportion and design, c.1830. Elegant and small, yet comfortable, this type of chair has become understandably very popular since the war of 1939 - 45. They are also to be found in rosewood, an even heavier and more durable wood which increases their value.

Price Range:	Single	£20 – £25
	Pair	£50 – £60
	Four	£150 – £200
	Six	£250 – £400

Value points: *Colour, patination and decoration (brass stringing etc.)* +++
Lightness of design +++

ref. **C1071 (77)**

A Regency period library chair which converts into a set of steps, c.1830. These chairs usually attracted a high degree of craftsmanship and are normally in either mahogany or rosewood. The arms and sabre front legs exhibit typical Regency characteristics although there is a hint of William IV in the broad carved top back rail.

Rather a hybrid piece of furniture which was either little made originally or subject to demolition from heavy bibliophiles. Either way, now becoming rarer and more expensive.

Price Range: £200 – £300

ref. **C1072 (78)**
A late Regency or William IV period chair made of mahogany, c.1835. In the heavy curl of the arms and the reeded front legs the approach of the Victorian era is foretold. The bold, wide, outward-pointing top rail is typical of the 1830 - 40 decade. Look out for conversion front legs, i.e. the original turned and reeded ones are sometimes removed and replaced by sabre legs to increase value.

Price Range: *Single Arm £20 – £30*
                     Pair   £60 – £80
                     Pair plus 2 singles £120 – £150
                     Pair plus 4 singles £200 – £250
Value points: *Balance of top rail ++ (heavy top rails detract).*

ref. **C1073 (79)**

Typical late Regency-cum-William IV rosewood single chair, c.1835. The front legs are octagonal in section and the design has become heavier. The drop-in seat is still light in character, however, and the classical influence still evident.

Price Range:
Single	£10 –	£12
Pair	£20 –	£25
Four	£50 –	£70
Six	£100 –	£120

C1074(80)

A country mahogany chair of the 1820 - 40 period. The Regency influence is evident in the arms, but the broad top rail belongs to the later part of the period.

Price Range: £20 – £30

ref. **C1075 (81)**

A Gillows chair of 1841 made for Colonel Cradock. The back shows a stage in design which precedes the balloon back, while the heavily turned and reeded legs of the period have been replaced by finely made and decorated cabriole legs. The seat rail has moved away from the Straight Regency design, and the total appearance is much lighter than the sub-classical designs of the 1820 - 40's. The top rail is undecided as to whether it is to follow the downward curve of the preceding example or to strike out into the new balloon shape. The French influence is also evident in the decorative effects.

Price Range: Single   £10 – £15
                 Sets   £15 – £20

ref. **C1076**

A mahogany chair of c.1845 with cabriole legs. The back is upholstered and its broad heavy top rail follows the late Regency trend, but the revival of rococo taste is evident in the scrolled feet and in the scrolling of the lower back rail. The legs do not show any decisive curving and mark that indecision of design characteristic of the period.

Price Range: £10 – £15 each
              In sets £15 – £20 each

ref. **C1077 (82)**

Balloon-back Victorian chair in walnut c.1850. The cabriole legs, despite a tendency towards bandyness, mark the distinct move away from the heavy turned legs of the previous years. The nicely proportioned curve of the seat rail between the legs helps to accentuate the change to a flowing, curved effect. These chairs were evidently very popular and were made for a number of years — perhaps up to the 1860's and in a modified form throughout the rest of the period.

Price Range: *Single chair*   £10 – £15
                 Sets of chairs £20 – £30 per chair

ref. **C1078 (83)**
Another mid-Victorian chair, c.1850, with cabriole legs and needlework back and seat. The legs are treated more slenderly, with less curvature and the scrolled knobs at the feet are less accentuated. The needlework, if original, adds to value.

Price Range:	Single	£10 – £15
	In sets	£25 – £35

ref. **C1079 (84)**

Early Victorian (1839) Gillows' chair with turned and reeded front legs. The downward curve of the thick top rail, which is carved, helps to produce a more integrated design. It is a sitting room chair with padded back to give additional comfort.

Price Range: Single   *£5 – £10*
                   In sets   *£15 – £20 each*

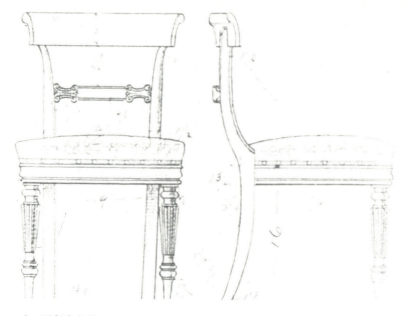

ref. **C1080 (85)**

A chair of a design normally associated with the William IV or early Victorian period. This is, in fact, a Gillows' design of 1877 and illustrates the fact that one must be very circumspect about dating Victorian chairs by their design, for one finds similar designs being executed over a period of thirty to forty years. The fully upholstered seat and moulded front rail give a heaviness not present in our William IV rosewood example, but the back and the turned and reeded front legs could easily be associated with the 1830 - 40 period.

Price Range: *Single*   £8 – £10
                     Sets of 4 or 6 £10 – £15 each

ref. **C1081 (86)**

An unashamed Victorian mahogany chair – c.1850 – of which the back owes much to the balloon design of more elegant versions. The uncorseted bulbous front legs are of a kind which have a robust appeal of their own, even though most dealers flinch at the sight of them.

Price Range: Single   £5 – £10
              In sets   £10 – £15 each

ref. **C1082 (87)**

Later period Victorian chair in mahogany. Note the heavier, squarer back with over-emphasized, eighteenth century style corner carving. The cabriole legs and seat rail are also heavily encrusted. The fully upholstered seat gives an appearance of overstuffing and top heaviness.

Price Range: Single £12 – £15
  Sets £15 – £20 each

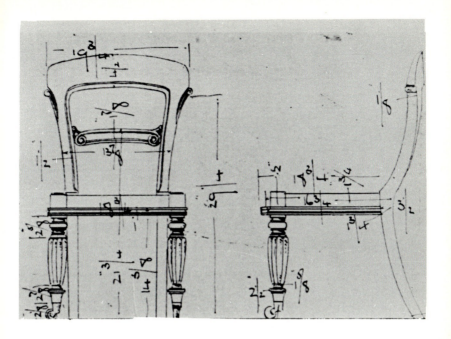

ref. **C1083 (88)**

A Gillows' design of 1884, which owes a good deal to fashions of an earlier period. The reeded legs are more bulbous and the upholstered seat — not shown in this constructional sketch — would be very full. The chamfered and grooved inside edge of the back is to lighten the effect of the very broad top rail and uprights. The latter have been ornamented with a small scroll at the join of the top rail, which almost seems an afterthought of design.

Price Range: Single   £5 – £10
                Sets   £8 – £10 each

UPHOLSTERED CHAIRS

Value points: Early examples with original upholstery, even if in worn condition, command a premium over the range quoted, often by an appreciable amount if the work is of fine quality. The position is reversed in the case of Victorian chairs where the upholstery is usually of ordinary quality. Clearly, most purchasers would pay a premium for new, good quality material.

ref. **UC1100 (89)**
Early eighteenth century – c.1720 – wing armchair with cabriole legs in walnut. Upholstered in leather. This is a fine example and well illustrates the three dimensional quality of the design. The wings sweep into the arms of this fine quality chair, which is as comfortable to sit in as one might imagine. Note the shape of the back legs; this feature was not normally well imitated by later craftsmen.

Price Range: £250 – £400

ref. **UC1101 (90)**
George II period – c.1740 – mahogany chair with stuffed back and saddle-shaped seat. Covered in Soho tapestry woven with birds and small landscapes in broad naturalistic flower borders; on scrolled cabriole legs.
Price Range: £150 – £200

ref. **UC!102 (91)**

A George III wing armchair upholstered in leather — c.1770. Note the square stretcher and leg construction of 'Chippendale' design. The curve of the wings is pleasant but the arms are a little stiff.

Price Range: £200 – £300

N.B. As these chairs command high prices there is a grave temptation to make a set of legs in the Georgian style and cover the modern frame with leather. Such examples usually lack the fluency of curve which was found in better class examples. A good dealer will leave the underneath uncovered to show genuine period features.

ref. **UC1103 (92)**

A later George III period – c.1790 – mahogany wing armchair. The sweep of the curve formed by the wings and the back rail is important. Compare the straight high line of the wings and arms in this example with the fluency of the two previous examples. This example is also rather thin, lacking the generous proportions of the better quality chairs. The lines would be improved by upholstery but the basic quality is lacking. The legs are tapered, ending in casters.

Price Range: £60 – £90

Value points: Line of back, arms and wings ++++
Design of legs+++

ref. **UC1104 (93)**

A Chinese Chippendale mahogany armchair with upholstered back and arms, c.1760. The bamboo motif is evident. The front legs are a remarkable achievement of craftsmanship and the nicely-scrolled brackets add considerable balance. The upholstery covering is of typical period design. The legs are of clustered column design.

Price Range: £450 – £600

ref. **UC1105 (94)**
Mid-eighteenth century chair in mahogany showing Chippendale construction in legs and stretchers, c.1760.

Price Range: £100 – £200

Value points: Carving or moulding on legs +++
              Originality of casters +

ref. **UC1106**

A later eighteenth century chair, probably c.1795, with leather upholstery, on turned legs. The shaping of the back still follows the 'saddle' style of UC1102, but the chair is cruder and the legs date it much later.
Price Range: £100 – £140

ref. **UC1107 (95)**
An open giltwood armchair – c.1760 – with considerable Adam influence in the frieze and fluted legs.
Price Range: £400 – £500

ref. **UC1108 (96)**
A George III period – c.1780 – open armchair with arched stuffed back and padded arms on curved supports with anthemion carving, the moulded frame with bead carving, the stuffed seat on turned tapering reeded legs with lotus leaf feet.
Price Range: £300 – £400

ref. **UC1109 (97)**

A later eighteenth century open armchair of French influence, but actually of a type made also by Chippendale, c.1780. The decoration includes cartouche backs headed by shell cabochons. The frame is carved with leaf mouldings, the scrolled arms with leaf shoulders. Covered in later gros-point needlework with panels of flowers in key-pattern frame against a blue ground with roses.

Price Range: £500 – £600

ref. **UC1110 (98)**
Regency period chair decorated with brass or painted gilt mounts, frequently ebonised.

Price Range: £20 – £40

Value points: Brass decorations ++
*   Well curved leg with stretcher +*

ref. **UC1111 (99)**

Bergere caned chair of Regency period, in rosewood, c.1830. These well made chairs have increased in popularity over recent years.

Price Range: £25 – £45

Value points: Brass decorations +
*   Rosewood ++*

ref. **UC1112**

A more elaborate bergere chair of Victorian character, c.1850. In this case the cabriole legs and scrolled arms are in the same style as upholstered armchairs of the period. The back has a very pronounced rake to it and the top rail sweeps boldly to a small scroll at each end. This example is in Virginian walnut and has a certain American air about it — possibly because ranch or railroad bosses of the Lee J. Cobb variety always seem to be sprawling in them on the screen. A loose cushion, possibly covered in hide, would have been fitted in the seat.

Price Range: £35 – £60

Value points: Decorative carving ++
Condition of caning +

ref. **UC1113 (100)**

A mid-Victorian open armchair in walnut, of the popular button-back type, c.1850. The fluency of the curve between the arm supports and the cabriole leg is spoilt by the thickness of wood at the point where the scrolls are carved. Most examples are better balanced. This example is in walnut, but many were made in mahogany.

Price Range: £50 – £70

Value points: Decoration +
Rosewood +

ref. **UC1114**

A mahogany button-back armchair of c.1850. The influence of rococo styles is clear in the carving and scroll feet. Possibly some of the later French Empire influence, prevalent in the 1810 - 1840 period, continued into the Victorian era without too much adulteration.

Price Range: £35 – £50
Value points: Carving +++
*   Cabriole legs +++*

ref. **UC1115 (101)**
A Victorian button-back mahogany 'ladies' chair, with cabriole legs, c.1850. The top rail is decorated with leaf carving. The 'grandmother' equivalent of the previously illustrated 'grandfather' (i.e. with arms).

Price Range: £30 - £50

Value points: Decoration +
　　　　　　　Rosewood +

ref. **UC1116 (102)**
Later Victorian upholstered chair on mahogany cabriole legs, c.1870. One of a large number of similar designs which, being very comfortable, have doubled in price over the last few years.
Price Range: £30 – £50

ref. **UC1117**

Another mahogany button-back armchair of c.1850, this time with turned legs. The arm supports are scrolled and so is the back. When the Victorians took to turning, they were predictably complex and the addition of reeding on the legs was often, as in this case, irresistible to them. Turned leg examples of this kind of chair never reach the same value as cabrioles.

Price Range: £25 – £40

Value points: Carving ++

ref. **UC1118**

Bentwood rocking chair, c.1850 onwards. The bentwood type of furniture was exhibited by the Austrian, Michael Thonet (1796 - 1871), in London in 1851. Large quantities of these popular rocking chairs were made during the 1860's and onwards, to the joy of modern architects, who seem unable to resist them for their own home decoration. The sweep and curve of the lines are, of course, extremely pleasing. Some were ebonised and both cane seats and upholstered ones were available.

Price Range: *£20 – £35*

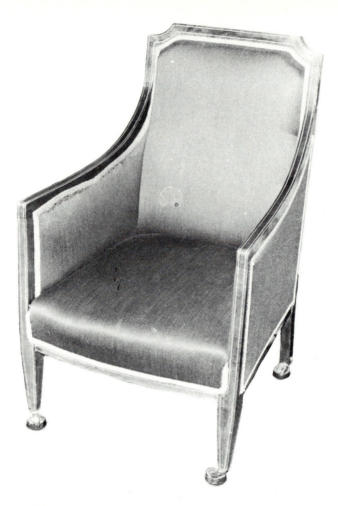

ref. **UC1119**

A restrained mahogany armchair of the 1890 - 1910 period which, again, demonstrates the return to eighteenth century styles. The square tapering legs and inlaid stringing lines, together with the square back design, relate to Sheraton examples.

Price Range: £20 – £35

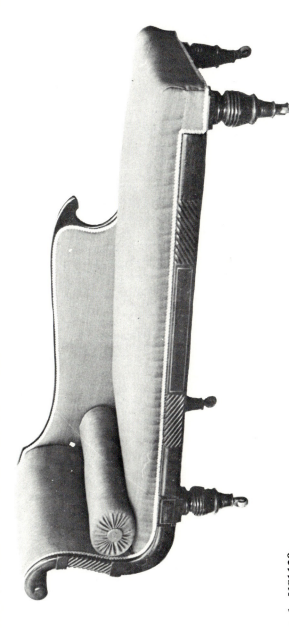

ref. **UC1120**

A mahogany Regency chaise longue of c.1820 on turned legs. The Empire styles of France contributed largely to the design of such pieces, which were also made with cabriole, sabre and square tapering legs, ending in spade feet. Upholstery condition plays an important part in price as with all sofas.

Price Range: *Before upholstering £20 – £30*
Upholstered in good quality velvet £40 – £80

Value points: *Carving +++*
Walnut ++
Cabriole or sabre legs +++

ref. **UC1121**

A Victorian walnut chaise longue of c.1860 on cabriole legs. In this case the back is button upholstered with just a single wooden scroll to the back, repeating that of the front arm and leg. A fairly grand specimen, upholstered in velvet, which would tend to be more decorative than utilitarian. Probably designed as part of a matching suite of arm, nursing and dining chairs.

Price Range: *Frame before upholstery* £30 – £40   *Value points:*   *Cabriole legs* +++
                Upholstered in good quality velvet £90 – £120   *Carving* +++

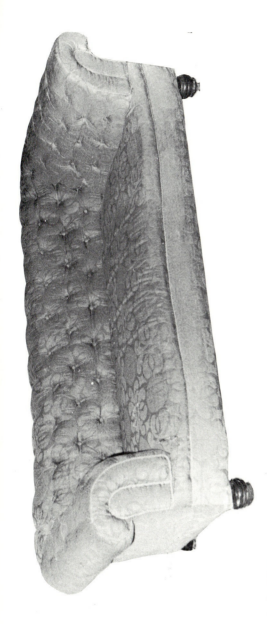

ref. **UC1122**

A Victorian button-back Chesterfield sofa of c.1870. The legs are turned and dark brown varnished. In the case of this type of fully upholstered piece it is the quality of covering and interior upholstery which dictates the finished price. Size is not always a contributing factor, but small examples tend to be slightly preferred.

Price Range: *Frame before upholstering £20 – £30*   *Value points: Small size ++*
  Upholstered in leather £150 – £200
  Upholstered in good quality velvet or similar £90 – £110

N.B. This type of sofa was made throughout the nineteenth century and reproduced on to the present day.

WINDSOR CHAIRS

Windsor chairs, or stickback chairs as they are more properly called, were probably first made in the early part of the eighteenth century. Principally they were a cheap form of seating useful for public assemblies, taverns, kitchens and the houses of the less prosperous. There are, however, some fine quality examples in existence which suggest that the virtues of the chair were appreciated by the more well-to-do also.

Early examples of Windsor chairs, particularly those with cabriole legs at front and back, have become expensive. Any Windsor chair with yew wood used in it moves to the top of the price range and there were some made in mahogany, which usually indicates better quality. The run-of-the-mill chair usually has an elm seat and legs. The yew chairs normally have elm seats also.

The same designs were copied for many years and dating a chair can, therefore, be extremely difficult. A late nineteenth century chair made in an earlier style, but hard used and polished for eighty years, is virtually unidentifiable from the earlier version. The heavier turned legs and arm supports one normally associates with the Victorian chairs were not always irresistible to the Victorian chair maker.

The principal chair making area seems to have been High Wycombe in Buckinghamshire, but chairs of individual design were produced in other parts of the country.

It is worth noting that sets of Windsors do not attract a premium price per chair over a single, to the same extent as other chairs.

ref. **WC1130 (104)**

A Windsor chair of c.1760. The seat would be very ample and the chair of bold proportions. Note the curving crinoline stretcher between the front legs — a feature usually associated with better-made chairs.

Price Range: Single   £60 – £90
*   In sets   £90 – £120 each*

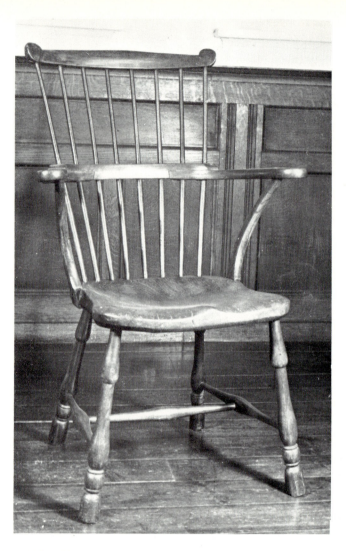

ref. **WC1131 (105)**

A comb-back Windsor chair of approximately 1780. Note the well-shaped saddle seat and the leg turning which is emphasized at the lower part. Many American Windsor chairs are of this design.

Price Range: *Single £30 – £40*
  (Yew not often found in this design)
  Also, sets of this type are not usually found.

ref. **WC1132 (106)**

Eighteenth century Windsor chair. Difficult to date exactly since this type was made for a long time, but probably late in the century and continuing into the early nineteenth century. The simple stickback without a splat, and the saddle seat are typical of the earlier types. The curving arm supports are also interesting, since during and after the Regency period turned arm supports became the fashion. This indicates that this chair may be earlier. However, this design appears in Gillows' cost books in the early nineteenth century both in mahogany and an elm and cherrywood combination.

Price Range: £25 – £40 *Elm and Cherrywood*
£40 – £60 *Yew*

ref. **WC1133 (108)**
A fairly common type of low-backed Windsor used for dining purposes. Note the turned arm supports which indicate nineteenth century origins.

Price Range: In yew £40 – £60
Other £30 – £40

ref. **WC1134 (109)**
A child's Windsor chair with the Gothic arched back in yew wood. Although the arm supports and legs bear fairly representative nineteenth century turning work, the crinoline stretcher and well shaped splat make this a nicely proportioned and well made chair.
Price Range: £40 – £50

ref. **WC1135 (111)**

A fairly typical Windsor chair of the nineteenth century. The proportion and the turning of legs and arm supports are altogether heavier. There are still reasonable numbers of these chairs in existence and their very strong construction, particularly when yew is used, makes them very durable and utilitarian antiques.

Price Range: *£50 – £60 when yew present*
                    £30 – £40 otherwise

ref. **WC1136 (112)**
A mid-nineteenth century Mendlesham chair of c.1830, a Suffolk variation of Windsor designs rather allied to Lancashire chairs in the decoration. Highly priced in East Anglia.
Price Range: £50 – £60

ref. **WC1137 (113)**
A late nineteenth century development of the Windsor chair. Rather ornate with heavy turning; simpler versions were common in schools and offices or institutions until recently.
Price Range: £15 – £20

ref. **WC1138 (114)**
Another simple variation of a type which was made during the latter half of the nineteenth century. In this case there is no left arm since the chair was made for an Officers' mess where the facility to rise, wearing a sword, without picking up the chair as well was a considerable advantage.
Price Range: £10 – £15

ref. **WC1139 (115)**

The Smoker's Bow, a chair very common in offices and public houses from the end of the nineteenth century onwards. A large heavy chair which will stand considerable abuse. The horizontal hoop is no longer made by bending the wood but is constructed from several pieces shaped on a band saw and screwed together. In early Windsor chairs this method of forming the hoop was adopted, but not always by using screws; the upright spindles did this.

Price Range: £4 – £10

DINING TABLES

The earliest form of dining table was a simple trestle type usually made of oak with an elm top. More solid forms of table appeared later, developing into the drawer and refectory tables of the sixteenth and seventeenth century. The early forms of refectory table had large bulbous carved legs which became more refined as the seventeenth century wore on. From the middle of the seventeenth century onward more types of table became available, starting with the gate-leg.

The early forms of gate-leg table were fairly crude and simple, with column turning of the legs, whereas later ones had more elaborate turning and turned stretchers instead of square ones. Since the gate-leg form continued on through the eighteenth century it incorporated successive styles: mahogany replaced oak and walnut, cabriole legs appeared and the top was held down by screws from the underframing instead of being pegged through the top. A great many mid-eighteenth century gate-leg mahogany tables had turned legs ending in pad feet, or later, square section legs of 'Chippendale' type.

Perhaps the most popular form of dining table in the Georgian period however, was the one composed of two 'D' ends which could be put together or have one or more leaves inserted between them to increase size. Each D-end however had to have at least four legs and like the gate-leg, these get in the way of those of the people seated at the table.

A radical improvement came with the use of a pedestal for each end or simply in the centre of the table. Double-pedestal dining tables and centre pedestal dining or breakfast tables are for this reason so justifiably popular now.

Victorian centre pedestal tables continued this usefulness while incorporating all the design trends of the period. In the Regency period the use of rosewood had become very popular as well as mahogany and the Victorians used these woods and walnut as well. Until comparatively recently these Victorian centre pedestal tables were very good value, but they have risen enough in price to check their original desirability.

Value points: The following value points must be taken to be common to all the examples illustrated:-

1. Top Surface. The first thing to strike the eye is the condition, decorative appearance and patina of the table top. The use of figured

woods and the condition of the top surface are vitally important; the better these are, the more the +++ factor will apply.
2. Structural Condition. We have again assumed this to be good.
3. Legs. Depending on the period, the design and proportion of the legs constitute an important factor in the assessment of a table. Legs are of course always liable to damage and their originality with the above points constitutes a +++ factor.

ref. **DT1200 (117)**
An early oak table of refectory type, c.1600. The large turned legs are connected almost at floor level with heavy stretchers. The main under frame is tenoned into the square tops of the legs and the table top consists of three or four massive oak planks. The main under frame provided a frieze for decoration and was often richly carved. The top was held in position either by under battens or oak dowels driven through the top into the under frame.

Price Range: £200 – £400. Depending on decoration and size. Larger tables are in the higher range.

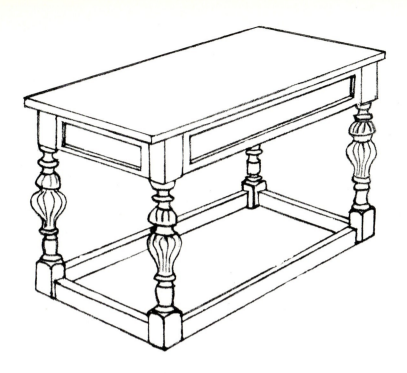

ref. **DT1201 (118)**

A slightly more developed small oak table of the early seventeenth century, c.1630. The turned legs are less bulbous than those seen on earlier tables and the frieze provided by the under frame is panelled, to allow for decoration. The fluting of the legs started to replace the bulb type in late Jacobean times and remained in use until after the Restoration.

Price Range: 6 seater £120 – £150
                8 seater £150 – £200

Value points: *Quality of carving and reeding of legs +++*
                Quality of carving of frieze ++++
                Thick top ++

ref. **DT1202 (119)**

Mid-seventeenth century oak table — c.1650 — with column turned legs, (sometimes called gunbarrel type). The floor-level stretchers are still evident and the top is made of three thick solid planks. The frieze is quite plain.

Price Range: *£120 – £180*   *Value points: Quality of turning of legs ++*
                                                    Size: – the greater the seating capacity, the higher the range.

GATE-LEG TABLES

ref. **DT1203 (121)**

One of the chief innovations of the Stuart and Commonwealth period (1603-60) was the gate-leg table. It appeared in Jacobean times but was perhaps not fully developed until after 1650. The turned leg was predominantly a Commonwealth innovation and the plain column turning

shown in the example above is typical of the period although the design continued for many years. Early gate-leg tables were made of oak, walnut or oak with elm tops. The example above is the latter. There are about twelve different types known, some being very rare. The number of legs varied from four to twelve and size from very small side tables to fully-blown dining tables to seat twelve people. The stretchers on many were left square, as above, with the two top edges relieved by a slight bead mould. On other and richer examples, the stretchers were turned, not always to match the legs. All framing joints are mortice and tenon with oak dowel pegs: in the mahogany gate-leg tables of the eighteenth century the joints were not pegged, as glue was then used and framing was cramped while it set. If design and size permitted a drawer was fitted set in the under framing, having a special carriage and runner made of a horizontal slat of oak, fixed longitudinally in the drawer space. The bottom of the drawer then slid on this; side bottom runners are known, but are rare. The top centre section was held on by oak or walnut dowels until the eighteenth century, when screws were put through the underside of the framing to secure it.

Price Range for illustration: £120 – £180

Value points: 6 seater ++
                8 seater +++
                12 seater ++++

ref. **DT1204 (122)**

Late seventeenth century oak gate-leg table — c.1690 — of fairly small dimensions, which could seat four people. Note the bun-shaped feet and the more developed turning of the legs.

Price Range: £70 – £90

Value points: Quality of turning on legs ++
*   Size: – again larger tables to seat more people gain value probably following:-*
*   6 people ++*
*   8 people +++*
*   12 people ++++*

N.B. This criterion does not apply to very small gate-leg tables for side use, which command a high premium.

ref. **DT1205**

Small oak gate-leg table of c.1670, with column turned legs but ending in square feet with a slight outward splay instead of the turned feet of our other examples. This is a simple table with plain, square section stretchers between the legs. The joint between the flaps and centre section is of the tongued and grooved type which was superseded in the eighteenth century by the rule joint.

Price Range: £60 – £80

Value points: Quality of turning ++
               6 seater ++
               8 seater +++
               12 seater ++++

ref. **DT1206 (123)**

Late seventeenth century gate-leg table in walnut, c.1690. Note the unusual features of turned stretchers and different turning of gates and centre section legs.

Price Range: Walnut   £150 – £200
              Oak   £100 – £120

Value points: *Quality of turning ++*
  6 seater ++
  8 seater +++
  12 seater ++++

ref. **DT1207 (140)**

George I period mahogany drop-leaf gate-leg dining table, c.1725. The scrolled cabriole legs show the hoof foot with which the cabriole leg was originally associated, being derived from an animal form. Tables of this type, with less refined form of leg, leading to the square 'Chippendale' type as with chair development, continued to be made well on towards the end of the eighteenth century.

Price Range: £200 – £250 *(for example illustrated)*

Value points: *Quality of legs +++*
              6 seater ++
              8 seater +++
              12 seater ++++

ref. **DT1208 (145)**
George III period square drop-flap mahogany gate-leg table, c.1760, with scrolled cabriole legs ending in ball and claw feet. The moulded edge of the table top is unusual and is similar to that found on some Victorian tables, with the exception that this is bolder but still detracts from the appearance.

Price Range: *£140 – £180*
Value points: *Quality of legs ++*
4 seater +
6 seater ++
8 seater +++
12 seater ++++

ref. **DT1209 (147)**

George III period oak gate-leg table with tapering legs ending in pad feet, c.1765. A type of table made for a considerable period throughout the mid and late eighteenth century. This example is exceptional in size and therefore the centre section is particularly wide.

Price Range: £50 – £70

Value points: Mahogany +++
6 seater ++
8 seater +++
12 seater ++++

(As an indication, this table, seating fourteen or more could be put in a range of £220 – £250).

ref. **DT1210 (152)**

Mid-Georgian drop-leaf table in mahogany of the gate-leg type, c.1760. The solid mahogany tapering legs end in pad feet. The main frame was often made from pine or else from oak and the centre flap secured to it by screws let in at an angle from underneath. A particular weakness with these tables is at the ends of the rule joints between flaps and centre, where part of the joint tends to split off. They make useful dining tables for the small modern home, since they can be folded away but their one defect is that of all gate-leg tables; there tend to be too many legs under the table when in use.

Price Range: £50 – £75
Value points: 6 seater ++
8 seater +++
12 seater ++++

ref. **DT1211**

A mahogany gate-leg drop-flap table of c.1770. The 'Chippendale' influence has produced the square section legs chamfered down the back edge. The wood is still a rather heavy Cuban mahogany with good figure, now rather faded. There are still no drawers in this table which is a pleasingly simple design. The majority available are suitable for seating six people but, occasionally, larger versions are to be found. Again these tables are subject to damage at the rule joints due to dislocation of the hinges and one should look for patching at the top and flap edges at the joining edge.

Price Range: £40 – £60

Value points: Figured woods ++
  Fading ++

ref. **DT1212**

A mahogany dining table of c.1790 consisting of two 'D' ends with a single leaf supported between them. This was one of the most common forms of dining table and in many cases could be further extended by some patent or ingenious means. The example above shows square tapering legs ending in spade feet. The top edge is reeded and there is a stringing line around the bottom edge of the frieze but otherwise this is a very simple example on which the legs are perhaps a bit heavy. Many of these tables have been broken up to form two 'D' tables for hall or console use.

Price Range: £50 – £75 *(for example above)*
             Decorative, cross-banded, inlaid examples: £200 – £300
Value points: *Decorative woods and inlays +++*

ref. **DT1213 (164)**

A fine mahogany dining table of c.1800 on turned columns each with three curved legs. The sweep of the latter from the central column out to the brass casters is particularly elegant. On such tables the centre section is generally bolted to the end pieces.

Price Range: £600 – £750

Value points: Elegance of columns +++
               4 seater +
               6 seater ++
               8 seater +++
              12 seater ++++
                Lightness of design ++

ref. **DT1214 (172)**

A Regency period dining table, c.1815, on two columns, again each supported by three elegantly curved legs. The apron frieze under the two end sections tends to add weight to the overall effect and breaks the line.

Price Range: £300 – £400

Value points: Elegance of columns +++ Lightness of design ++ Seating capacity 4 + 6 ++ 8 +++ 12 ++++

176

ref. **DT1215 (173)**
Regency period dining table, c.1820, in mahogany on two turned columns each supported by three curved legs. The shaping of the turning on the columns suggests a later part of the period, as do the legs, but the top is reeded round the edge and light in appearance.

Price Range: £300 – £400

Value points: Elegance of columns +++ Lightness of design ++
Seating capacity 4 + 6 ++ 8 +++ 12 ++++

ref. **DT1216 (182)**

Regency period breakfast table in mahogany, cross-banded with kingwood, c.1825. The octagonal column is on a platform supported by unusual curved and shaped legs ending in brass paw casters. The spur shape on the knee of the legs is particularly unpleasant.

Price Range: £300 – £350

Value points: Seating capacity 6 ++ 8 +++

ref. **DT1217**

A mahogany breakfast table of Regency design, c.1830. Like all breakfast tables this one is designed to tip up and can thus be put to one side after use. The top is a single piece of mahogany of a size capable of seating six people and has an inlaid black stringing line inset two inches from the edge, which is reeded. The point of a single-piece top is important, for tops made from two pieces tend to separate over the years, and it is often difficult to re-glue and cramp the halves together again successfully.

The base shows the departure from restrained Georgian forms to scroll-like knee pieces of concentrically ringed effect. Generally a heavy 'knee' like this indicates Regency or later periods.

The example here is a fairly simple one without the cross-banding or inlays of more exotic versions. At present price ranges are fairly wide for these tables which are clearly appreciated for their excellent use as a dining table.

Price Range: £130 – £250
Value points: *Cross-banding +++*
                 Inlaid stringing ++
                 Curl or figured woods +++

ref. **DT1218 (184)**

Large Regency period dining table, c.1835, of extendable type with leaves which are inserted in the centre section to provide greater seating capacity. A type of table now somewhat reserved for board rooms and public banqueting halls but which nevertheless follows the development of the earlier Georgian type with two 'D' ends between which leaves could be inserted. This table would seat approximately twenty people. The legs are spirally reeded.

Price Range: £110 – £150. **N.B.** It is interesting to note that ten years ago such tables were hard to sell and often cut up for the good quality wood of which they were made.

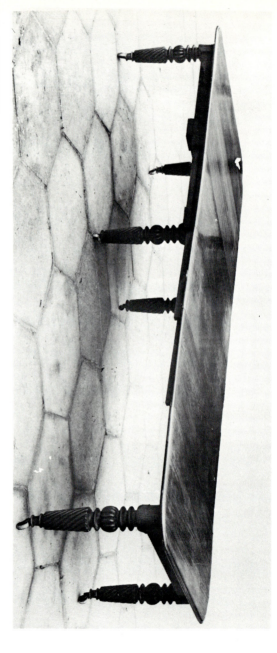

ref. **DT1219**

A Regency period rosewood circular table of c.1830. The top is veneered in highly figured rosewood with a broad decorative brass inlaid edge banding. An apron or frieze, cross-banded in rosewood beneath the top adds weight and proportion to it. The triangular base supports the curved triangular column which also includes a brass stringing line and exhibits a bead mould at the base joint. The base is on spur sabre-type legs ending in brass paw casters. Altogether a high quality example.

Price Range: *£250 – £300*

Value points: Quality of brass inlay +++

ref. **DT1220**
A Regency period rosewood circular dining table of c.1825. The top is veneered in figured rosewood and the centre pedestal is geometrical in section. The rather heavy but simplified base is typical of this type of table which has increased greatly in popularity and price in the last two years. Usually these tables are of the tip-up type.
Price Range: £50 – £75
Value points: Carved base +++

ref. **DT1221 (206)**

An early Victorian – c.1850 – circular dining table of a type found in both mahogany and burr walnut veneer. The tripod carved base with its leaf, scroll and paw foot carving shows great exuberance and quality of execution, even though our artist's lack of serious feeling for the period has given the impression that the piece is on its way to the chiropodist's. It is an example of good Victorian cabinet work.

Price Range: £75 – £100

Value points: Quality of carving +++
 6 seater ++
 8 seater ++++

ref. **DT1222**

A late Victorian or Edwardian mahogany dining table, c.1870 onwards. The square cornered influence of the late nineteenth century gives rise to a mixture of designs which wholly fail to blend.

Price Ranges: £20 – £30

Value points: Mahogany ++

Examples are frequently to be found in oak and American walnut.

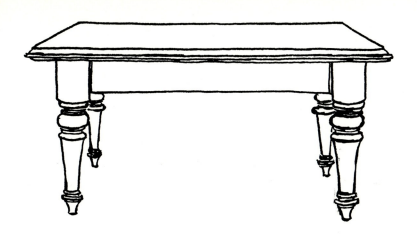

ref. **DT1223 (208)**

A mahogany late Victorian dining table with the heavy underframe and ponderously turned bulbous legs. The top is usually made of two or three leaves and the table can be of the extending type. Note that the edge moulding has become rather over-emphasized.

Price Range: £10 – £25

Value points: Quality of leg turning +++
Figured woods +++

SIDE AND CARD TABLES

Probably one of the most collected forms of antique furniture is the occasional side table which is both decorative and sometimes functional. Early forms of side table of the seventeenth century are perhaps a little too heavy, being mainly made of oak in ponderous design, but from the late seventeenth century onwards many delightful forms of games and side tables in prevailing fashions were produced.

Value points: The common value points for examples illustrated are:

1. Top Surface. The first thing to strike the eye is usually the condition, patina and decorative figuring or inlays of the top surface. The more perfect and decorative this surface is, the more the +++ rating will apply.
2. Structural Condition. This must again be good, particularly where folding tables are concerned. The Georgian and Regency card tables usually had side hinges to the folding top and these are often the cause of damage, leading to unsightly patching, replacement and alteration. The legs and stretchers, if applicable, must be sound.
3. Legs. Depending on the period, the design and always the proportion of the legs must constitute a very important factor in the assessment of a side or games table. Carving on cabrioles, or moulding of straight legs, affects value. Legs are, of course, always liable to damage and their originality with the above points, constitutes an +++ factor.
4. Handles. Where a drawer or drawers are involved, original period handles constitute a ++ factor.
5. Shape. Later Georgian folding card tables on tapering square legs in designs generally associated with Hepplewhite and Sheraton are affected by an important factor: the shape of the top. If this is circular when open, i.e. half round when shut, a +++ factor may be assumed. Tables which are oval, or with geometrical straight sides do not attract as high a price. On these tables cross-banding of the square tapering legs constitutes a +++ factor.

ref. **ST1250 (120)**
Mid-seventeenth century oak side table, c.1650, with two drawers in the frieze. Note the panelled shape of the drawer fronts, reminiscent of chests of drawers of the period. The turned legs and square stretchers are still retained.
Price Range: *£120 – £150*

ref. **ST1251 (124)**

Small oak side table, c.1675. The simple column turning of the legs and the stretchers is of the same type as the gate-leg table illustrated earlier. The top is fixed to the framing with oak dowel pegs. The two drawers fit tight under the top without a lock rail in the framing. Note that there are now simple bun-like feet under the square leg-stretcher joints, which lift the stretchers slightly higher off the floor. On original undisturbed pieces the dowels protrude above the level of the surface (stand proud).

Price Range: £60 – £90
Value points: *Quality of leg turning* ++

ref. **ST1252 (127)**

Walnut side table of the post 'Restoration' period, c.1680. The twist turning so popular to the Restoration period continued to be used on the legs and stretchers of tables though simple turning still persisted. Walnut was by far the most favourite wood though oak by no means went out of use. While the legs and bun feet are solid walnut, the top and drawer fronts are veneered. The veneered stretcher is 'Y' shaped at each end, connected by an oval widening — intended for a bowl. It is more common to have one drawer only and the best examples would be inlaid with marquetry panels.

Price Range: *Marquetry £400 – £600*
                              Walnut   £350 – £450
                              Oak   £80 – £120

ref. **ST1253 (128)**

Country side table in fruitwood of William and Mary period. The baluster turning of the legs shows later characteristics but the country maker has retained the square stretchers and construction from an earlier period. Note the drawer fitting tight under the lock rail and the square, pegged tenon joints. This type of table was made well on into the late eighteenth century.

Price Range:	£60 – £90
Value points:	*Walnut ++++*
	Fruitwood +++

ref. **ST1254 (125)**

A William and Mary period side table, c.1690, of a type generally found in walnut, but also frequently decorated with marquetry. The serpentine X stretcher is also found on earlier tables, but the inverted cup form on the turned legs is more generally associated with William who brought over Dutch craftsmen from whom this form originates. The legs would be in solid walnut whereas the top, sides, drawer front and stretcher would be veneered.

Price Range:	Marquetry	£400 – £600
	Walnut	£350 – £500
	Oak	£90 – £120

ref. **ST1255 (126)**

ref. **ST1255 (126)**

A solid walnut side table of William and Mary period, c.1690, with arched shaping of the frieze below the drawer. The X-shaped stretcher is well illustrated and the heavy turning and bun feet are typical. Note the thumb-nail top edge moulding.

Price Range: £250 – £300

Value points: Proportion and quality of leg turning +++
Shaping of frieze ++

ref. **ST1256 (129)**

A William III side table, c.1700, inlaid with seaweed marquetry. The thumb-nail moulding is ebonised. The double-scroll legs of square section are particular to this period and not to everyone's taste, but the stretcher form and flat bun feet are typical. Seaweed marquetry of this quality demanded a high degree of skill and such pieces are increasingly rare.

Price Range: £500 – £750
Value points: Quality and area of decoration ++++

ref. **ST1257 (130)**

William and Mary period carved wood table, c.1690, decorated with gilt and gesso. The decoration of furniture by gesso was done in order to economise in carving by giving a pattern in slight relief without the need to carve it. It was a rich man's style and comparatively small quantities were made, chiefly small tables and mirror frames. The style appears to have had a relatively short duration, from 1700 to 1735.

Price Range: £250 *upwards.*

ref. **ST1258 (131)**

A William III Walnut Card Table, c.1700, the oval folding top veneered outside and inside with burr-walnut, cross banded and with herringbone lines, the shaped frieze with three small drawers, on six tapering octagonal legs including two rear gate-legs, united by stretchers, and with turned feet.

Price Range: £1,500 – £2,000

ref. **ST1259 (134)**

A card table of Queen Anne period with fine cabriole legs, c.1710, ending in ball and claw feet. The knees show the shell and pendant husk motif, having a C scroll on the inside edge. Note the shaping at the corners. The usual covering was green velvet or a plain polished wood surface as above. The method of extending the table, which folds to a side table when not in use, is of the 'concertina' action type. The cabriole legs are 'hipped' at the top i.e. continue above the line of the frieze in a scrolled shape.

Price Range: £1,000 – £1,500

Value points: Quality of hipped cabrioles, shell motif, bold ball and claw feet +++

ref. **ST1260 (135)**

Another walnut card table, c.1720, of the early eighteenth century with graceful cabriole legs decorated with shell motif on the knee and ending in ball and claw feet. The shaping for candle stands at the corners is clearly shown, as are the inserted cups for counters.

Price Range: £1,000 – £1,200

ref. **ST1261 (138)**
A George I mahogany card table, c.1725, showing the candle stands and cups for counters similar to the walnut tables of an earlier period. The bold cabriole legs end in ball and claw feet and the shaped frieze has an echo of the shell motif about it. Tables of this kind in mahogany continued to be made into the second quarter of the eighteenth century.
Price Range: £180 – £250

ref. **ST1262 (139)**

A George II period card table, c.1730, in mahogany with shell motif on the cabriole legs. The shaped corners for candle stands are retained but the frieze is straight.

Price Range: £175 – £250

ref. **ST1263 (141)**
A Virginian walnut table of c.1720, with fine cabriole legs ending in spade feet. This table has lost its folding top but the centre drawer and shaping of the frieze are similar to earlier types. A provincial or country made version of the finer examples.

Price Range: £150 – £250 (with folding top)

ref. **ST1264 (142)**

A George I period table, c.1725, in oak, the tapering legs ending in pad feet. A side table which could be put to use for cards or other occasional use. The space behind the frieze is used for storage. The top flap has clearly been damaged at the side hinge and reversed to hang down behind the table. Originally it would have been flat, on the top of the table.

Price Range:	Oak	*£100 – £125*
	Walnut	*£280 – £340*
	Mahogany	*£200 – £250*

ref. **ST1265**

A George II period games table, c.1730, in mahogany with turned tapering legs ending in pad feet. The inner right-hand back leg is on a gate which swings out behind the table to support the top when the upper flap is opened over by means of its side hinges to produce the circular games top. This inside surface is usually covered in baize, with a broad crossbanding produced by the baize being inset into the surface. The lower flap also opens on side hinges to give access to the deep storage space behind the frieze, where gaming materials are kept. The table is a natural stylistic evolution of the walnut one ref. ST1258, and examples in solid and veneered walnut were made. Cabriole legs were also employed on same example. Note the slightly overlapping shaping at the top of the legs, sometimes extended to form a 'fold' at the top of the leg. The inside surfaces sometimes have 'cups' scooped out of them for holding the gaming counters as shown on ST1260 and ST1261.

Price Range: £200 – £250

Value points: Cabriole legs +++
*   Fold on legs ++*
*   Virginian or 'Red' walnut +++*
*   Counter Cups ++*

ref. **ST1266 (144)**

A George II mahogany side table, c.1740, elaborately carved on the frieze with a lion mask and acanthus leaves. The cabriole legs have lion masks carved on the knees with ribboned flower heads and terminate in ball and claw feet. The top is a marble slab.

Price Range: £750 – £1,000 for a single table

ref. **ST1267**

A George II, c.1740, folding top table in heavy mahogany. The cabriole legs ending in pad feet are a modification of earlier cabriole legs in that the earlier exuberance has been curbed and the leg is now much more restrained. These tables were probably multi-purpose, being used for both games and for refreshments such as tea. The left-hand back leg is on a gate, to swing open to support the top when folded over in the open position. Side hinges allow this folding action and, as with all card tables, tend to be a point of weakness or breakage over the years.

Price Range: £120 – £150
Value points: Figured woods +++

ref. **ST1268**

Later Georgian side table of c.1760. The 'Chippendale' straight chamfered leg has replaced the earlier pad feet. The top edge still shows a variant of the thumb-nail moulding but is heavier. As well as being chamfered on the inside the legs show a 'scratch' moulding down the front corner, as seen on chairs, to give a further lightness to the effect. By now, the lock rail is evident under the top and the drawer thus comes below this. Country versions might still omit the lock rail however and have pegged tenon joints.

Price Range: £40 – £60 (mahogany)

ref. **ST1269 (148)**

Later Georgian c.1770 side table similar to the previous example, with elm top and fruitwood legs. Note there is no lock rail under the top. The square Chippendale style legs are chamfered at the back and the front corners have the scratch moulding down the edge to lighten them. The drawer front is elm.

Price Range: £35 – £45

ref. **ST1270 (154)**

A 'Chippendale' folding card or tea table in mahogany with moulded square legs, serpentine front and elegantly shaped frieze, c.1760-70. Tables of this kind are always higher in value if of the 'tea' type, i.e. with solid wood surface on the interior, rather than 'card' type with a baize interior.

Price Range: £175 – £225
Value points: 'Tea' type ++

ref. **ST1271 (153)**
A George III, c.1765, country solid walnut side table on tapering legs ending in pad feet. The flap is supported when open by a gate leg. The top and flap are made of several planks.
Price Range: £30 – £50

ref. **ST1272 (155)**
A very fine quality Chippendale card table c.1770. The edge of the frieze is gadrooned and this effect is followed down the corner edges of the legs. The edge of the top is also carved. The wood is mahogany. The legs are chamfered on the inside.
Price Range: £250 – £300
Value points: Quality of carving +++

ref. **ST1273 (156)**
A Chippendale mahogany card table, c.1760, with a green baize lined folding top. The edges, frieze and square chamfered legs are fretted in the Chinese manner, which inexplicably makes this normally rather underpriced piece of furniture double its value.
Price Range: £150 – £200
N.B. Without this fretwork a plain card table of this type is now £40 – £50 The 'tea' version with polished interior is £60 – £70.

ref. **ST1274 (158)**

A mahogany circular folding table of c.1790 with Hepplewhite-cum-Sheraton influence in the design. A type which could be used as a games or tea table, the latter usually being claimed when the inside is not lined with baize but veneered in the manner of the outside. The stringing lines add considerable elegance as do the oval medallions in the panels at the top of each leg, which ends in a spade foot.

Price Range: *£140 – £180*

Value points: Matched figuring of mahogany and stringing +++

ref. **ST1275 (159)**

A George III satinwood and marquetry card table, c.1790, with a folding circular top, cross-banded with rosewood. The inlay consists of urns and flower festoons within a meandering band of anthemion and the frieze is similarly inlaid. The square tapering collared legs with the oval medallions at the top are of a kind generally associated with Shereton designs. These tables were frequently made in pairs.

It would be difficult to find more highly valued tables of this period.

Price Range: £850 – £1,000

Value points: Quality of decoration +++

N.B. Inferior Edwardian copies abound.

ref. **ST1276 (160)**
A Sheraton period (1790 - 1800) satinwood card table cross-banded with rosewood. Note the tapering legs and the medal set in the top panel of the leg.
Price Range: £200 – £250
Value points: Satinwood +++

ref. **ST1277**

A mahogany card table of c.1800 in figured veneer with square tapering legs, ending in spade feet. There is a simple boxwood stringing line around the top edges and the frieze which is repeated around the spade foot top. It is covered in baize inside and is not quite circular when open, although not exaggeratedly oval. Circularity is an important value point, however. This table has the advantage of a double gate, i.e. both back legs open outwards to support the folding top when open.

Price Range: £80 – £100
Value points: Decorative inlays +++
             Satinwood ++++

ref. **ST1278 (161)**

A Sheraton period (1790 - 1800) mahogany card table cross-banded with satinwood. Note again the oval medals at the top of the tapering legs and the inlaid stringing lines.

Price Range: £200 – £250

It is to be noted that a pair of identical tables causes the individual piece to be more than doubled. Thus a pair of such tables would be in the £600-£700 range.

ref. **ST1279 (162)**
A Sheraton period (1790 - 1800) mahogany serpentine fronted side table on tapering legs. An elegant design with interesting enlargement of the square section added as ornamentation near the bottom of legs.
Price Range: £100 – £120

ref. **ST1280 (183)**
Regency period mahogany card table, c.1820, on turned centre column. The hinged folding top pivots on the frame which forms the frieze to provide support when open. Note the fluted square leg forms.
Price Range £60 – £90

ref. **ST1281**

A Regency period – c.1820 – rosewood card table, with inlaid stringing and bead-moulded edge decoration. For some reason the semi-elliptical hoop support under the top and above the centre pedestal attracts a higher price from dealers than other types. A sofa table with a similar support is illustrated in the relevant section. Although the craftsmanship involved in executing this design is undoubtedly high, the overall effect is to produce a confusion of styles and a weakness of support.

Price Range: £130 – £170

Value points: Rosewood +++
Brass stringing +++
Original casters ++

ref. **ST1282**

A fairly typical Regency card table of c.1830 on a turned centre pedestal supported by four sabre legs. The fold-over top has a beaded edge moulding and swivels about the centre to allow support from the underframe when open. Inside there is a green baize covering.

Price Range: £100 – £150
Value points: Rosewood +++
*   Brass inlays +++*

ref. **ST1283**

A late Regency rosewood card table of c.1830. The top is inlaid with a brass border line and swivels across its underframing, which supports it when open. Bead moulding doubly decorates the frieze and the top edge of the base. It is an example of the revived rococo and conflicting designs of the period: paw feet; leaf decoration; turned, reeded and carved column; and a kind of cabochon-and-leaf corner decoration to the frieze, which is also concave.

Price Range: £60 – £80

Value points: Figured woods and inlays +++

ref. **ST1284**

A fairly typical plain mahogany card table of late Regency or early Victorian period, probably c.1840. The centre pedestal can be either circular in section, often of gunbarrel appearance, or octagonal, and the base usually reflects this in design. The top swivels and opens to form a baize-lined square surface.

Price Range: £30 – £60

Value points: Rosewood +++
               Figured woods and inlays +++

ref. **ST1285 (205)**
A Victorian folding walnut card-table, c.1845. Like the circular and oval dining tables of the period, it is thinly veneered in burr walnut and inlaid with marquetry patterns. The base is quite elaborately carved. Inside the surface is lined with baize.

Price Range: £25 – £40

Value points: Marquetry inlay +++

DRESSING TABLES

Towards the end of the seventeenth century the small tables in walnut and oak or country woods specifically designed as dressing tables made their appearance. Before that it seems to have been the practice to use a small side table with perhaps a small desk with sloping lid or mirror on it.

Since they were designed to be decorative as well as functional, dressing-tables have produced some of the most sophisticated and pleasant pieces of their periods. Their natural appeal to women of a much later period than those of that for which they were designed has always kept them to the forefront of demand.

Dressing tables of the walnut period exhibit all the most desirable features of walnut veneered furniture: quartered tops with herringbone cross-bandings; cross-grained mouldings; turned legs with early forms and stretchers or, later, cabriole legs with scrolls, and so on. As a microcosm of period features and because of their small size, they have become very sought after and hence very expensive.

The later eighteenth century dressing tables in mahogany and country woods make no less ideal collectors pieces and hence are also greatly in demand. So far Victorian examples have not followed the analogy of chairs and dining tables perhaps because the Victorians tended towards larger dressing tables without the same appeal.

Value points: The following value points apply to the examples illustrated.

1. Top Surface. As with other tables, the condition, patina and figuring of the top surface are important. The more perfect and decorative the appearance, the more the +++ factor will apply.
2. Structural Condition. This is again assumed to be good.
3. Legs. Depending on the period, the design, and always the proportion, of the legs is an important factor. Legs are always liable to damage and their condition and originality constitute a +++ factor if good.

ref. **DRT1300 (132)**

Small walnut William and Mary period dressing table, c.1690. The top would be veneered in walnut, quartered to give a symmetrical pattern from the figure, and with a 'herringbone' or 'feather' inlay around it, inside the cross-banding. The thumb-nail moulding around the top edge and indeed the decoration of the top is similar to chests of drawers of the period. A half-round moulding around the drawers is also typical. In the frieze it is usual to find a shallow centre drawer and two deep ones on either side, or two short drawers. The arched shaping of the frieze is typical. Drawer pulls are of peardrop shape in brass and on a circular or star-shaped plate, the handle being linked to a double strip of brass or iron which was passed through a small hole in the drawer front, parted, pressed down and pinned into the wood. The inverted cup form on the legs, as mentioned earlier, shows the Dutch influence, and the bun feet and shaped veneered stretchers are also typical.

Price Range: £400 – £600

Value Points: Decoration of top +++
 Proportion of legs ++

ref. **DRT1301 (133)**

A Queen Anne period dressing table and mirror set of c.1710 which are japanned in a light background with flower decoration. The table shows the typical arch shaping of the frieze and there are two acorn pendants on the centre arch. The octagonal legs taper down to turned shaping and bun feet. The 'X' stretcher with its scroll shaping has a central circular pedestal for a bowl. Note that the table top has a thumb-nail edge moulding and there is a half-round or 'D' moulding on the front around each drawer. The mirror is described in the Toilet Mirror section.

Price Range: £500 – £600

ref. **DRT1302 (136)**

Queen Anne walnut dressing table, c.1710. Note that the turned legs of the William and Mary period have now changed to cabrioles although the shaping of the frieze remains similar. The top edge moulding, veneers and drawer arrangement are still in the earlier style.

Price Range: £400 – £500

Value Points: Quality of cabriole legs +++
Original handles +

ref. **DRT1303 (137)**

Walnut dressing table, c.1720. The rather deep full top drawer gives a slightly top-heavy effect since the cabriole legs are rather slender. The top edge moulding is a refined thumb-nail type. The top veneer is quartered and cross-banded; the drawers are edged with cock-beading and have a feather or herringbone cross banding. The handles are not original. A poor photograph which makes the piece out of proportion.

Price Range: £350 – £450

ref. **DRT1304 (143)**
George I period dressing table in fruitwood, c.1725. The arched shaping of the frieze is similar to that of earlier periods, with the projecting lip moulding or cock-bead around it. The heavy thumb-nail top edge moulding of the earlier period is now more refined. The tapering legs ending in pad feet are simpler than the cabriole but retain an elegance and proportion of design in a particularly English leg form. The handles are not original.
Price Range: £150 – £200

ref. **DRT1305 (146)**
Oak dressing table of c.1740. The square section cabriole legs are still of slender shape but not the most desirable form, particularly if heavy. The shaping of the frieze has become much more sophisticated. Note the top edge moulding.

Price Range: £120 – £150
Value Points: Walnut ++++
　　　　　　　Fruitwood ++

ref. **DRT1306 (150)**
Later Georgian, c.1770, country dressing table in walnut and fruitwood. The three drawers in the frieze are cross-banded in fruitwood like the top, which is veneered in plain straight grained walnut. The legs are elm.
Price Range: £60 – £80

ref. **DRT1307 (163)**

A George III mahogany dressing table with square legs chamfered at the back, c.1770. An unpretentious table whose origins are clear from previous illustrations and of a type increasingly popular. The top edge still retains a moulding derived from the thumb-nail but now more sophisticated with an ogee curve.

Price Range: £60 – £80

ref. **DRT1308 (151)**

A later Georgian c.1780, country dressing table in oak. The frieze is shaped, but the slightly tapered legs hint at Hepplewhite influence. The drawers are cock-beaded and the top edge has a rather refined moulding. Tapering legs tend to be a later feature.

Price Range: £60 – £80

ref. **DRT1309 (350)**

A satinwood dressing table of Sheraton period, c.1795, with mirror which folds flat to lie under the folding top. Similar designs for shaving tables and lady's cabinet dressing tables of involved character are to be found, but this is one of the more popular designs of the period.

Price Range: £200 – £250

Value Points: Satinwood ++++
Original Mirror ++

ref. **DRT1310**

A mahogany dressing table of c.1820, with replacement handles. The square tapering legs and rectangularity of design reflect a Sheraton influence. The black stringing lines around the top and the drawers and frieze are often identified with this period. Useful also as occasional writing tables, these pieces are understandably popular, as well as having a simplicity of design which allows them to blend easily with modern decor.

Price Range: £40 – £60

Value Points: Figured woods and inlays +++

PEMBROKE AND SOFA TABLES'

Pembroke tables are said to be named after the Countess of Pembroke who first gave orders for one of them. It seems they first appeared about 1750 and were generally made in mahogany. They do not seem to have really caught on until after 1780, when they were made with square tapering legs and followed Hepplewhite or Sheraton designs. The flaps on either side are supported by hinged wooden brackets. A drawer is usually to be found opening at one end while a mock drawer is put at the other to give design balance.

Sofa tables are similar except that the flaps are at the ends of the table instead of the sides. Sheraton referred to the normal dimensions as being 'between five and six feet long and from twenty-two inches to two feet broad!' The most serviceable type have two drawers and they were frequently used to write, draw or read upon.

Value points:

1. Top Surface. The condition, patina and figuring of the top surface is very important. The more perfect and decorative the top surface, the more the +++ rating will apply. Exotic inlays and cross-banding in satinwood, zebrawood or other prized veneers usually constitute ++++ factors.
2. Structural Condition. Due to their rather elegant but more fragile construction, large numbers of Pembroke tables on the market have been damaged at some time or another. Usually it is a leg joint or loss of a caster which causes the trouble. The rule joints to the flaps should be examined for patching because these tend to be damaged in the same way as those on gate-leg tables. Prices shown assume sound structural condition.
3. Legs. Design and proportion of legs is important. On Pembroke tables, cross-banding of the square tapering legs can constitute a ++++ factor.
4. Drawers. A Pembroke table without a drawer — we illustrate one — is considered a severe disadvantage from a value point of view.

ref. **PT1350 (167)**

A country mahogany Pembroke table, c.1780, in heavy Cuban wood and with no drawer. The square chamfered legs owe more to the Chippendale influence than the tapering variety normally associated with this type of table. A simple and pleasing version.

Price Range: £40 – £60

ref. **PT1351 (168)**

A Thomas Sheraton mahogany Pembroke table, the top cross-banded with herringbone bands of kingwood, with a rising 'Harlequin' section with a fall-front inlaid with ribboned festoons of flowers in scorched and green fruitwood, in the manner of Pierre Langlois, the frieze with a drawer either side and simulated drawers, on square tapering panelled legs.

The design for this 'Harlequin Pembroke Table' was published by Thomas **Sheraton** as plate LVI in his *'Drawing Book'* (1791-94). In his notes he describes such table as "serving not only as a breakfast, but also as a writing table, very suitable for a lady. It is termed a Harlequin Table for no other reason but because, in exhibitions of that sort, there is generally a great deal of machinery introduced in the scenery". This type was also illustrated in Hepplewhite's *Guide*.

This table is of further interest in that the 'till' is inlaid with a floral garland, knotted with a ribbon-tie, in a marquetry of many woods. This is reminiscent of the highly distinctive style of inlay favoured by the emigrant French ebeniste, Pierre Langlois.

Price Range: *£750 – £1,000*

ref. **PT1352 (165)**

The example above of c.1790 date is perhaps one of the finest of the fine: in satinwood, with marquetry inlaid, and cross-banded with rosewood. It is on square tapering collared legs and the marquetry inlay consists of urns and naturallistic festoons of flowers.

Price Range: £500 – £750

ref. **PT1353 (166)**

Good quality Pembroke table in mahogany with cross-banded top edge, c.1790. The tapering legs end in elegant brass casters.

Price Range: £120 – £170

Value Points: Cross banding of top ++
                 Circular or oval shape ++++

ref. **PT1354 (169)**
A rather broad mahogany Pembroke table with slightly tapering legs of c.1790. The solid top is of a particularly finely figured wood and there is a broad boxwood stringing line under the cock-beaded drawer which is continued across the leg.
Price Range: £60 – £80

ref. **PT1355 (170)**

A Sheraton mahogany Pembroke table of c.1810. The square tapering legs have given way to the centre pedestal, the pillar of which is fluted. The four sabre style legs which support the platform at the pillar base have typical later Georgian and Regency brass casters of decorative style. The top is veneered in highly figured mahogany and cross-banded with satinwood, which is used for the inlaid decoration also.

Price Range: £275 – £325

Value Points: Inlaid decoration of high quality +++

ref. **PT1356 (175)**
A fine quality late eighteenth century – c.1790 – sofa table in mahogany and satinwood. The end supports, curving elegantly out from the vertical to end in brass casters, are particularly noteworthy.
Price Range: £500 – £700

ref. **PT1357 (176)**
Mahogany sofa table of later Georgian period, c.1800. The reeded curved legs on the end supports terminate in brass paw casters.
Price Range: £400 – £500

ref. **PT1358 (174)**

The sofa table above is of c.1805 date and has brass mounts and stringing. The inward curving legs are reeded. Rosewood and zebrawood were used for higher quality examples as well as mahogany. The addition of brass stringing or more detailed inlay in brass adds considerably to value.

Price Range: £400 – £500

Value points: Exotic woods and inlays +++

ref. **PT1359 (177)**

Regency sofa table, c.1810, in mahogany with lyre-shaped end supports. The top edge is moulded as well as cross-banded.

Price Range: *£400 – £450*

Note. The existence or hint of the lyre motif in any form inexplicably pushes prices to the top of the range.

ref. **PT1360 (178)**
Sofa table of slightly later date c.1810 with turned supports in conjunction with inward curving legs. This form of centre support is to be found on card and other tables of the period and is never valued as highly as the end-supported type.
Price Range: £280 – £350

ref. **PT1361 (179)**
Regency sofa table with gadrooned top edge, c.1820. The curving splayed legs on the end supports are reeded.
Price Range: £200 – £250

ref. **PT1362 (180)**

Regency rosewood sofa table, c.1820, the top and flaps cross-banded in satinwood. The stringing which can be seen round the drawer fronts is of brass, and brass stringing is also used on the top and in the unusual curving support and base. The table when extended is five feet long. The semi-elliptical support under the top is highly valued by dealers.
Price Range: £250 – £300

LIBRARY TABLES

Since a library was the possession of only rich men until the end of the eighteenth century, the tables designed for it were correspondingly lavish and were in the style of the famous designers. However, with the spread of wealth and the tendency of the new middle classes to set aside a study or room of books as a library, more pieces of furniture for such rooms were made. Tables were generally designed for working or writing upon and reflected contemporary styles.

Value points in common are the same as those for other tables, but concealed or false drawers may always be taken as +++ points.

ref. **LT1370 (185)**
Regency mahogany library or 'rent' table, c.1810, with leather-covered top. A type introduced in George III's reign which was made on into the nineteenth century, sometimes with an octagonal top. Used sometimes on estates where the relevant documents were kept in the drawers; hence the popular term 'rent table'.
Price Range: £400 – £600

ref. **LT1371 (186)**
Regency rosewood library or rent table, c.1810, with octagonal revolving top inset with tooled leather. The inlaid stringing lines are of brass.
Price Range: £500 – £600

ref. **LT1372 (181)**
Regency mahogany library or writing table, c.1830. A derivation in some ways of the sofa table. The end supports show in their design the influence of the lyre motif.
Price Range: £90 – £120

ref. **LT1373 (171)**

A library or writing table of c.1820 with turned legs on casters. The three drawers are cock-beaded and the handles are typical of those used from 1780 onwards. In this case the top is solid mahogany, but leather tops are also common.

Price Range: £60 – £90

ref. **LT1374**

A Victorian library table of c.1850 with a leather top. The table is of oak, with drawers at each end and false drawers in the frieze at the sides. The cabriole legs are carved with flower decoration at the knee and leaf decoration at the foot. Similar tables for library and writing use are made in mahogany or walnut.

Price Range: £65 – £90

Value points: Walnut +++
　　　　　　　Inlaid decoration +++

TRIPOD TABLES

The principal role of tripod tables has been as wine or occasional tables for social use. As a piece of furniture a tripod table of small size is decorative and useful in this respect, but easily knocked over and liable to damage. Many of the tripod tables for sale in shops nowadays are marriages of top and base from different origins for this reason. The tripod legs, keyed into the central column, are also easily damaged and the joint split due to an excessive weight being placed on the table. A metal spider is often screwed under the base to reinforce the legs against this.

The original method of securing the top was by two parallel bearers, hinged to fit on to the squared top of the stem. Sometimes a gallery or 'bird cage' was used and this, being regarded as a mark of quality, tends to add to price. By placing a weight too near the edge of the table it is possible to damage the top fixing also, and many of these have had to be repaired.

To detect a 'marriage', examine the underside of the top for old screw holes or marks of previous bearers. Although successful unions do take place, there is usually a loss of proportion and relationship between top and base. Do not be misled, in country versions, by talk of country craftsmen using one wood for the top, another for the stem and another for the legs. Although this may have happened, it was not nearly so widespread as the subsequent repairers would have us think.

Value in tripod tables is dictated by the same considerations as those of other furniture; quality of craftsmanship, proportion, colour and choice of wood, polish and patination. Above all, originality is to be prized as much as structural condition.

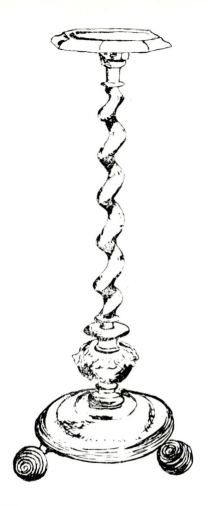

ref. **TT1380 (189)**

The tripod table is not strictly speaking derived from the candle stand in our illustration above, but it is possible to trace the influences derived from it. This stand, c.1670, is of walnut, and was made originally for holding a light. The octagonal top has a moulding round it which is typical of the late seventeenth and early eighteenth century walnut period, and the twist turned stem represents a high degree of technical accomplishment.

Price Range: £200 – £300

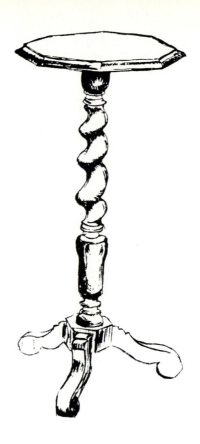

ref. **TT1381 (190)**

A walnut stand of the early eighteenth century. The octagonal top again has the moulded edge of the period and is veneered in figured walnut. The base of the stand is now lifted off the floor by the three curved feet of square section.

Price Range: £125 – £175

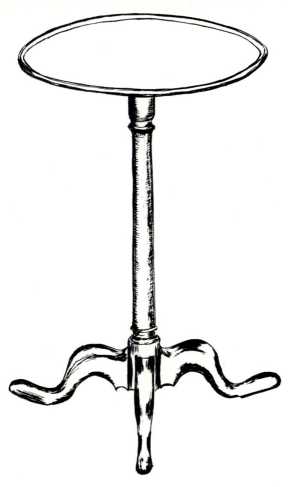

ref. **TT1382 (191)**
A mahogany tripod of mid-eighteenth century — c.1750. The top is dished to give the rim around it, and the plain column is of pleasing simplicity. The mahogany used is of the heavy Cuban variety, very dark in colour. Note the development of the height of the legs, becoming bolder.
Price Range: £60 – £80

ref. **TT1383 (192)**

A Chippendale style mahogany tripod table, c.1760. The top shows the 'pie-crust' edging which requires a high degree of craftsmanship, since the whole top is made in one piece. The stem is fluted down to the carved bulbous vase and the legs, with shell and pendant decoration on the knee, end in ball and claw feet. Note the scroll on the inside of the knee of the leg. One of the most ornate and decorated examples of this type.

Price Range: £500 – £800

ref. **TT1384**

A Mahogany tripod table of c.1760 with a 'bird-cage' gallery beneath the top. The pillar is a fine simple form and the bold set of the legs is typical of the better and earlier Georgian tripods. The use of the gallery construction ensures that the top can both tip up when not in use, and yet revolve when in the position shown. A wedge locks the top and gallery to the column, so that the removal of this wedge enables the whole top to be lifted off the base.

The best quality pieces have a top made from a single piece which preferably is dished to leave a moulded or 'pie-crust' carved edge (see Reference No. TT1383). The example above has a plain top but made from a single beautifully figured piece of mahogany. Originally used for tea or supper and for setting out the new china tea services.

Price Range: £70 – £90

ref. **TT1385 (195)**
Typical eighteenth century tripod table in mahogany, probably dating from 1760 - 80. The legs have now become almost aggressively higher and bolder in curve. The tapering column has the bulbous vase at the base.
Price Range: £30 – £50

ref. **TT1386 (196)**
Another tripod mahogany table of c.1790, with similar stem, but the legs now flattening in curve slightly. The rounded curves are modified by the chamfered edges and more pointed design.
Price Range: £20 – £30

ref. **TT1387**
A Georgian mahogany dumb waiter of c.1770, with finely crusted carved edge to each tier, and well-balanced pillar and vase shapes to the stem. Note the casters under the feet; a feature often found on dumb waiters since they were, of course, designed for movement like Canterburys.
Price Range: £150 – £250

ref. **TT1388 (197)**
Tripod table of c.1790, with baluster turned stem and chamfered legs.
Price Range: £30 – £50

ref. **TT1389 (198)**
Tripod mahogany table, c.1790, of larger dimensions – the top approximately two feet, nine inches in diameter. Note the spirally fluted vase at the base of the tapering column stem. Until recently these were more difficult to sell, being too large for occasional or wine table use. Now they are rising in price and being used as tea tables or small dining tables.
Price Range: £40 – £60

ref. **TT1390 (352)**

Late Georgian mahogany dumb waiter of c.1790, in which the upper tiers are of the folding flap type. Dumb waiters were used from the early eighteenth century onwards and were generally placed near a table so that guests could help themselves without the need for servants to stand in attendance. Sheraton includes them in his *Cabinet Dictionary* but the designs are rather complicated.

Price Range: *£120 – £160*

Value points: Elegance of tripod base +++

ref. **TT1391**

A mahogany tripod of later Georgian period, c.1815. Although the top is ten-sided, the column and base are turned, with the column showing the slightly baluster form and triple bead of 'bamboo' effect. At this stage the tripod legs have become highly arched and curved, in a manner somewhat reminiscent of early eighteenth century designs.

Price Range: £25 – £35

ref. **TT1392 (199)**

Fruitwood tripod table, twenty-seven inches in diameter, c.1800. Note the rather abbreviated feet and the fact that it has been necessary to use several planks to make the top, due to the lack of width in fruitwood trees.

Price Range: £30 – £50

ref. **TT1393 (200)**

Yew wood tripod table, c.1800. The legs are better proportioned than the fruitwood example, although they show the steep outer curve of the later period. The top again is several planks, but yew is a wood which is always more highly valued.

Price Range: £60 – £90

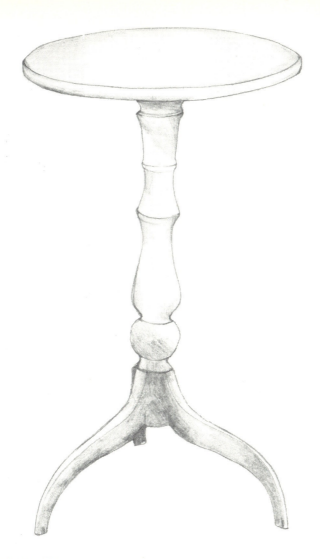

ref. **TT1394 (202)**
Early nineteenth century country tripod table in mahogany, c.1820. The legs are in the reverse type of curve, but the stem shows the rather bulbous turning that heralds the Victorian period.
Price Range: £10 – £20

ref. **TT1395 (203)**

Early nineteenth century tripod table with rectangular top, c.1840, of a type expanded in size to produce a breakfast table. This smaller size could be used as a supper table and, being of the tip-up type, was useful in smaller rooms. The wood is generally mahogany and the legs and stem exhibit the same characteristics as dining tables of the period.

Price Range: £60 – £80

ref. **TT1396**

A mahogany ex-tripod table of c.1840, with hexagonal column. The top is veneered in plain mahogany on pine, but the column is solid. The tripod base has now become a flat one like others of the period, without legs and raised on turned knob feet.

Price Range: £7 – £12

Value points: Decorative woods +++

ref. **TT1397 (204)**

Later nineteenth century version of the tripod table — c.1860. The tripod legs have actually vanished and all that remains is the triangular shaped flat base with its three turned feet. The stem is now thoroughly overturned with far too many bulbs and vases.

Price Range: £7 – £12

ref. **TT1398**

A papier-mache tea table of c.1850, japanned and painted and with mother of pearl inlay. The baluster turning of the column is fairly typical and although this example has taken a list to starboard, some idea of the decorative value can be obtained. The outer painted decoration and that on the column and base, now faded, were originally gilt.

Price Range: £40 – £60

ref. **CT1399**

A cricket table. There are various theories as to why they are so-called, but it is most probable that they were used in village pubs on the green, where one could sit watching the game. They were made in oak or elm, from the eighteenth century onwards.

Price Range: £20 – £30

CHESTS AND CHESTS OF DRAWERS

The earliest form of chest was a simple coffer-like construction with solid sides reaching to the floor to act as feet. By the seventeenth century, a joined frame construction with panels had appeared, and these panels, and also sometimes the hinged lid, were decorated with carving and even inlays. The evolution of the clothing used in the later part of the seventeenth century made it undesirable to keep heaping clothes on top of each other inside these pieces, and drawers appeared insides to separate them.

The chest of drawers is said to have appeared about 1650, and the first form was half chest and half cabinet. Usually there was one deep drawer either in the upper or lower part, and shallower ones enclosed by doors. The drawers were grooved in the sides to run on bearers fixed to the carcase until after the Restoration, when bottom drawer runners appeared.

On the early types the fronts are often decorated with mitred geometrical mouldings and split balusters. Inlays of bone, ivory and mother of pearl are to be found on the more important pieces. With the advent of walnut fashions towards the end of the century, much more sophisticated and decorative chests of drawers appeared, usually on stands with twist or cup-form legs. The bun foot used on such chests gradually gave way, in ordinary chests, to bracket feet and to those on stands to the cabriole leg, so popular in the first half of the eighteenth century. Oak continued to be used during the evolutionary period of walnut from 1670 - 1730, after which mahogany became much more general, except in country pieces, which were made in a variety of woods.

Value points:

Oak Period (to 1690). Value points are given individually for early oak chests. For chests of drawers, however, the following points must be taken as common to all examples:-

Colour and patination +++
Original feet +
Original handles +

Walnut Period (1670 - 1740). In chests on stands, the existence of an original stand gives a ++++ factor. (The legs, stretchers and feet on such stands have nearly always been replaced due to damage and rot).

Marquetry ++++
Choice of veneers, figures and patination +++
Original brass handles and keyhole plates +++
Faded cross-grain mouldings in short lengths ++
Veneered top (on chests or stands) +++ (this was left unveneered on pieces originally over about five feet, six inches high).
Veneered and cross-banded sides ++ (country pieces left sides oak or pine, and the side mouldings were cut along the grain instead of across it).
Oak drawer linings + (country pieces usually lined in pine).
Original bracket or bun feet +
Size: For chests of drawers, or chests on stands the following notation applies:-

        3' 0" wide or under ++
        2' 9" "   "   " +++
        2' 6" "   "   " ++++

Quartered top +++. The best quality chests of drawers had the tops veneered in four matching pieces to form a fine formal pattern in veneers. Lesser quality pieces sometimes had the top veneered in two matching halves, while country pieces sometimes had one plain sheet of top veneer.
'Feather' or 'herringbone' inlay or cross-banding ++

Mahogany Period (1730 onwards). In mahogany examples the following points may be taken as commonly affecting value:-
Choice of wood and figure +++
(Early Spanish mahogany or decoratively figured wood add greatly to the price).
Original handles and keyhole plates ++
Oak linings +
Serpentine bracket feet on later examples +
Colour and patination +++
(Faded mahogany is considered particularly desirable).

Size: 3' 0" wide or under ++
              2' 9" "   "   " +++
              2' 6" "   "   " ++++

For all chests, it may be taken that structural condition and originality are important value points.

ref. **CH1400**

One of the earliest forms of chest is illustrated above. This type is usually smaller than the panelled type and was made from the fifteenth to the seventeenth centuries. The sides are made of a solid plank, carried down and shaped to form feet. The front, back, lid and bottom are also usually made of one plank each; oak is normally the wood used, but elm and sometimes chestnut were used also. The gouge cuts across the corners, giving a serrated effect, are typical and so is the arched carving, similar to lunettes, but carving was often added by later 'improvers'. The brackets across the corners of the feet on the front are not common. The fixing was either by large iron nails or oak dowel pins. Chests of this kind were still made after the panelled and joined type appeared in the sixteenth century.

Price Range: £30 – £60
Value points: Quality of carving +++

ref. **CH1401 (211)**
Early seventeenth century oak chest - c.1630 - with three front panels decorated with stylised geometric carving. The rails are also carved with an arched pattern typical of the period. On this chest the plain solid sides are of walnut, which was much more commonly used than is generally supposed, but of which less survived than oak, due to its greater susceptibility to woodworm.

Price Range: £60 – £90

Value points: Depth, intricacy and profusion of carving +++
The addition of human faces, figures ++++
Coats of arms ++++
Dating and initials (if genuine) ++

ref. **CH1402 (212)**
Mid-seventeenth century oak chest with panelled front, top and sides, c.1650. The front panels, stiles and rails are carved in fairly shallow decoration of a botanical nature. The escutcheon plate has been added later.

Price Range: £40 – £70

Value points: Quality of carving +++

ref. **CH1403**

Oak chest of c.1650 with four plain panels to the front and two in the lid. The moulding around the edges of the stiles and rails, next to the panels, is typical, and helps to relieve the squareness of the construction. The end framing is carried down to form feet and a moulding is carried down the length of these ends. The construction is by mortice and tenon joints which are secured with oak pegs or dowels without any glue being used.

Price Range: £35 – £50   *Value Points:*   *Carving* +++   *Inlays or decoration* +++

ref. **CH1404 (214)**

Mid-seventeenth century plain oak chest with three undecorated panels in lid and front, c.1650. Ornamentation of the frieze by carving is typical of these pieces and known as strapwork.

Price Range: £30 – £40

Value points: Decoration ++
               Dating ++
               Coats of Arms ++++

Warning: These simple chests were often 'improved' in the Victorian period by elaborate carving; in an attempt to simulate age, the quality of the carving looks very amateur.

ref. **CH1405 (215)**

Later seventeenth century oak chest, c.1670, with single drawer beneath; the evolution of the chest of drawers is commencing. The split baluster decoration and the mouldings are similar to those found on chests of drawers.

Price Range: £60 – £90

Value Points: Quality of mouldings and decorations +++

ref. **CH1406 (217)**

An early eighteenth century — c.1720 — oak chest, with two drawers under, sometimes known as a mule chest. It shows the transition from a simple lidded chest with three fielded front panels to a chest of drawers. At some stage bracket feet have been added as can be seen on the right hand foot, but originally it seems to have been on straightforward 'stump' feet, formed by carrying the end frame down to the floor. The moulding around the drawer fronts suggest that it does not precede 1700, although chests of this type appeared in the seventeenth century.

Price Range: £25 – £50

Value points: Inlays or decoration +++

ref. **CH1407 (218)**

Early eighteenth century chest, c.1730, veneered in walnut of high figure on an oak carcase. It is decorated with herringbone inlay. There are carrying handles at each end; the base is separate.

Price Range: £110 – £150
Value points: Figure of walnut +++
Trunk lid ++++

ref. **CH1408 (219)**

Mid-eighteenth century elm country chest, c.1750, of simple construction from solid planks. Integral base and bracket feet. Common side dovetails show on the front face. Made from the eighteenth on into the nineteenth century.

Price Range: £15 – £20

Value points: Mouldings around lid and base ++
Figure and grain of wood +++

ref. **CH1409 (220)**

Typical early form of chest of drawers, c.1670, with panelled cupboard doors. The split turned decoration applied to the front and sides and the turned bun feet indicate a date of c.1660 - 70.

Price Range: £100 – £140

Value points: Quality of decoration and mouldings +++

ref. **CH1410 (221)**

Late seventeenth century – c.1680 – oak chest of drawers often misnamed Jacobean. Note the simple mouldings and fielded panelling of the drawers. The chest is made in two halves for ease of transportation. The bun feet are typical of the William and Mary period. The drawers run on side rails on a rebate in the thick drawer linings, which are normally in oak. The thin top has a thumb-nail lip edge moulding. The handles are original.*

Price Range: £100 – £150

Value points: Veneered panels in other woods +++
Intricacy of mitred drawer fronts ++
Applied split baluster decoration ++
Decorated inlay ++++
Original feet ++

*Note the deep second drawers.

ref. **CH1411 (222)**

A late seventeenth century oak chest of drawers, c.1690, similar to the previous example. The mitred drawer fronts are more decorated and the balance of the piece is lighter. There is a convex moulding under the top and the carcase frame continues down to form the feet; a feature of an earlier period. The knobs are not original.

Price Range: £90 – £120

Value points: Veneered panels and inlaid decoration ++++

ref. **CH1412 (223)**

William and Mary walnut chest on stand. Cross-banded drawers and top with inlaid stringing line. Note early period thumb-nail top edge moulding. Half-round moulding on carcase front, c.1690.

Price Range: £350 – £450
Value points: See section notes

ref. **CH1413 (224)**

William and Mary Period — c.1690 — oyster and marquetry chest on stand of superb quality. The twist turning which remained so popular after the Restoration is well illustrated in the legs. The flat, shaped stretcher is veneered in walnut on the top face. The mouldings are first class examples of the cross-grained type of the period and the thick inlaid boxwood lines are bold examples of the type. Note that the sides are also veneered and inlaid with boxwood stringing. A half round moulding on the carcase front follows the drawer edges.

Price Range: £800 – £1,200

Value points: Quality of marquetry decoration +++

ref. **CH1414 (226)**
William and Mary oak chest on stand, c.1690, with drawers cross-banded in walnut. The projecting lip moulding, rather like a cock bead, around the shaped frieze of the base, is a feature found on dressing tables of the period. Note the double D moulding on carcase front around the drawers.
Price Range: £160 – £190
Value points: Drawers cross-banding ++

ref. **CH1415 (227)**
A very fine William and Mary period – c.1690 – chest of drawers in oyster veneer, decorated with stringing lines in geometrical patterns. The wood used is laburnum, which gives a rich dark colour with a hard, close grain. Even the half-round carcase edge mouldings around the drawers, the crossbanding and the top and bottom edge ogee mouldings are in this wood, but the bun feet are probably walnut. Note that the sides are also decorated in the same manner as the top.

Price Range: £500 – £750
Value points: Quality of decoration +++
　　　　　　　Decorated sides +++

ref. **CH1416 (228)**

William and Mary period – c.1690 – chest of drawers veneered in laburnum oyster pieces. Possibly Anglo-Dutch due to low positioning of locks and the thin drawer linings. Top veneered in concentric circles of oysters. Sides also veneered in oysters with wide cross-banding. Width 3ft. Note heavy top edge moulding similar to thumb-nail and half-round or 'D' moulding on carcase front around drawers. Cross-banding of drawers, top and sides in laburnum also. Handles not original.

Price Range: £350 – £450

Value points: Colour, patination and oyster pattern +++

ref. **CH1417 (229)**

Early walnut chest of drawers – c.1700 – inlaid with stringing lines in boxwood. Note heavy thumb-nail moulding around edge of top echoed in the moulding around the base above the bracket feet, possibly originally on low stand as feet are not original. The grain on original veneered feet is usually vertical, both to follow the direction of the grain on the drawer front and because if it were cross-ways the veneer would chip off more easily. Half-round of 'D' moulding on carcase fronts around drawers. All mouldings cross-grained and in short lengths.

Price Range: £250 – £350

Value points: Quality of decoration +++

ref. **CH1418 (230)**

Queen Anne period chest on stand, c.1710. Note the fine cabriole legs and shaped base. Carcase fronts now flat veneered – no moulding – and drawers have ovolo lip moulding around edges to 'lip' over carcase front. Drawers cross-banded.

Price Range: Walnut £350 – £500
                 Oak   £150 – £250

Value points: In walnut: Quality and originality of cabriole legs +++
                In oak: Colour and grain ++ Medullary rays across drawer fronts tend to detract from value. Drawer cross-banding: If in walnut or fruitwood ++ Mahogany (after 1730) + Many country versions have no cross-banding or ovolo moulding on drawers.

ref. **CH1420 (231)**

Queen Anne period chest on stand in walnut veneer, c.1710. Note that the cabriole legs have the shell motif on the knee — a mark of quality — and web feet, an unusual feature also of quality. The piece is boldly proportioned with shaped frieze to the stand, half round or 'D' moulding on the carcase front around the drawers and a simple cross-banding. All the mouldings are cross-grained and of good proportion.

Price Range: £350 – £500

Value points: Quality and originality of cabrioles +++

ref. **CH1419 (232)**
William and Mary period – c.1690 – walnut chest of drawers on bun feet, (not original). Inlaid with boxwood stringing lines in geometric pattern on top. Possibly placed originally on a low stand. Note the deep top edge moulding is more towards Queen Anne type but half-round or 'D' moulding on carcase fronts remains. Fairly straight-grained veneer but sides veneered and cross-banded. Top quartered.

Price Range: £250 – £350

Value points: See section notes

ref. **CH1421 (233)**

Walnut chest on chest, c.1730, with half herring-bone cross-banding on drawers. Bottom drawer has curved centre panel inlaid with 'sunburst' and waved apron. Top and bottom halves with chamfered and fluted corners. Bracket feet. Veneer fairly straight in figure and grain; carcase fronts veneered and drawers lip-moulded on edges.

Price Range: £300 – £400

Value points: Size 6' 6" high or under ++
                 Sunburst in bottom drawer +++
                 Chamfered and fluted corners ++

ref. **CH1422 (234)**

A Queen Anne period or possibly George I chest on chest or 'tallboy' in walnut veneer, c.1705. In this example there is an ovolo 'lip' moulding around the drawer edges to lap over the flat veneered carcase front edges when closed. The drawers are not actually cross-banded; an inlaid stringing line around the drawers, suitably inset from the edges, gives this effect. Note that the bracket feet are also veneered in the same vertical figure arrangement as the front of the piece – restorers sometimes forget to do this when replacing feet. The sides are veneered, with a cross-banding down the vertical edges only – a feature common to these pieces. The top moulding shows the concave cavetto form.

Price Range: £350 – £500
Value points: As for other chests

ref. **CH1423 (235)**

Country walnut chest on stand, c.1715. Ogee type top edge moulding; half-round or 'D' moulding on carcase edges around drawers. Note the 'half-herring bone' cross-banding around drawers i.e. the cross-banding is at forty-five degrees – a cheaper variation of the full herring-bone or 'feather' type cross-banding. This type of cross-banding was used on country pieces until a later date, running concurrently with full herring-bone; it is easier and simpler to produce. The square-cut cabriole legs are rather clumsy – those on the illustrated piece are not original. The top is not veneered and it has plain pine sides and drawer linings. The handles and escutcheons are period reproductions. Walnut veneer has some figure but the piece has poor patination. A patch in the veneer can be seen on the second long drawer in the top half, on the left hand side.

Price Range: £150 – £250

Value points: See section notes

ref. **CH1424 (236)**

George I period walnut bachelor chest of drawers, c.1720. Note evolution of a slightly later period in chests of drawers in the flat veneered carcase fronts and the drawers with cock-beading around the edges. Herring-bone or feather inlay in the drawers gives a cross-banded effect. Size approximately 2' 3" wide by 2' 8" high by 1' 0" deep. Drawers oak lined.

Price Range: £1,000 – £1,500
Value points: See section notes

ref. **CH1425 (237)**

A walnut bachelor's chest of c.1740, the drawers having cock beading and herring-bone or 'feather' inlay. The top is cross-banded and again has a herring-bone inlay between central panel of veneer and cross-banding.

Price Range: £1,000 – £1,500

Value points: See section notes

ref. **CH1426 (238)**

A mahogany bachelor's chest, c.1750, the design following quite plainly the earlier walnut type. The folding top is simple and solid, without an edge moulding.

Price Range: £450 – £600

In this case the fading and figure of the mahogany are particularly remarkable, and would constitute +++ points.

ref. **CH1427 (239)**

A walnut chest of c.1740 date, decorated with inlaid boxwood stringing to give a cross-banded effect. The small double lip moulding around the drawers, on the carcase fronts, is a later refinement of 'double D' mouldings of an earlier period. The top edge moulding is also a Georgian refinement. It is interesting to note the three small top drawers, usually a warning that the piece has been on a stand, but in this case the veneered top could be an indication that this need not be so.

Price Range: £150 – £175
Value points: Quality of decoration +++
Veneered sides ++

ref. **CH1428 (240)**

Walnut chest of drawers of later period, c.1740 - 50, country made. The drawers are pine lined. The thin top edge moulding gives an example of later lack of boldness and the original double 'D' moulding around the drawers has been replaced by a single 'D' which is a little too clumsy at this width. Drawer fronts veneered in plain straight-grained walnut with little figure. Cross-banding of drawers is 'half-herring-bone', i.e. at forty-five degrees which is typical of country pieces which emulated an earlier period. The top quartered and cross-banded in plain walnut. This piece has added interest in that the sides, instead of being plain pine or oak are, in fact, solid walnut (+ factor).

Price Range: £110 – £150

Value points: Treatment of sides i.e. Veneered ++ Solid Walnut ++

There are still plenty of these chests about but beware many 'improved' or recently veneered country pieces.

ref. **CH1429 (241)**

Mahogany chest of drawers on bracket feet, c.1755. A thin thumb-nail top edge moulding round the top is echoed by the ovolo lip moulding around the drawers. A very typical example of mid-eighteenth century chests of fair quality and which are also found in oak and pine with occasional country variations.

Price Range: £60 – £80

Value points: Figure of wood ++
(Faded mahogany is popular)

ref. **CH1430 (242)**

Mid-eighteenth century mahogany chest of drawers, c.1760. The four graduated drawers are cock beaded around the edges. The deep ovolo top edge moulding is repeated in the moulding around the base, above the shaped bracket feet. The figure of the wood is dark and rich. Original swan-neck handles.

Price Range: £80 – £100

Value points: Size width. 3' 0" or under ++
2' 9" or under +++
2' 6" or under ++++
Figure of wood ++

ref. **CH1431 (243)**

A mid-eighteenth century chest of drawers, c.1760, of high quality; of a design normally found in mahogany. Bold top edge moulding; brushing slide; chamfered and fluted sides; a fine graduation of drawer sizes; all indicate the quality of the piece. The bracket feet are boldly shaped and the plain 'swan neck' handles are contemporary. Note the replacement of escutcheon plates by the thin threaded key hole fittings.

Price Range: £150 – £200

Value points: Brushing slide +++

ref. **CH1432 (244)**

A mahogany serpentine-fronted chest of drawers of c.1755. The shaped drawer fronts are veneered, with a cock-beaded edge. There is a brushing slide and the decorated handles are of fine quality, matching the piece. An important point is the feature of the canted corners faced with a blind fret in Gothic pattern. Similar chests which merely come to a point at these corners do not assume nearly the same value. The sides of this chest are straight but if they were shaped a further addition to value would be involved. These serpentine chests are nearly always of a larger character and the general rule of small size equating with higher value need not necessarily apply.

Price Range: *£500 – £750*

Value Points: *Brushing slide ++*
                 Canted corners with fret +++
                 Pronounced mouldings +
                 Boldness of Serpentine front +++
                 Shaped sides +++

ref. **CH1434 (251)**

Simpler mahogany tallboy, without brushing slide and with a plain frieze under the cornice. Chamfered and reeded sides to the top half and ogee bracket feet add quality to this example, c.1760 - 70.

Price Range: *£100 – £125*

Value points: Chamfered and reeded sides ++
*   Ogee bracket feet ++*

ref. **CH1435 (252)**

More ornate mahogany tallboy, with dentil moulding; the frieze under it is decorated with a blind fret pattern. The reeded pillars let into the sides have decorative brass mounts and the finely figured drawers have a crossbanding inside the cock bead. Ogee bracket feet complete a high quality example, c.1760 - 70.

Price Range: £200 – £250

Value points: Decoration and carving +++
Dentil frieze and blind fret ++

ref. **CH1436**

Two of the most difficult items to value nowadays are the clothes press and the wardrobe. Due to the understandable preference for built-in cupboards and modernity in the contemporary bedroom these bigger pieces have often become difficult to dispose of. The example above is in fact a fine quality piece and for that reason would command a high price in a specialist market. The plainer examples are not so easy to sell. The top half, originally lined with shelves, does not provide sufficient hanging room for dresses and coats so that a modification frequently carried out has been to remove the top two small drawers from the chest section to provide extra hanging space. When this is done the drawer fronts are rebuilt in as false ones and only the bottom two long drawers remain as genuine ones.

The clothes press above exhibits the characteristics of the 1760 period well. There is a dentil frieze under the top moulding and the doors are panelled and cross-banded. The drawers are cock-beaded and oak lined, with original 'swan-neck' drop handles. The bracket feet are, of course, a standard feature. Normally these pieces are made in mahogany, the plain ones solid and the better quality ones veneered with feathered figuring or special effects and possibly inlays. Exotic woods, however, were also used and add to value.

Price Range: *High quality (as illustrated) £250 – £300*
Plain mahogany £25 – £50

ref. **CH1437 (248)**

Mahogany chest on chest of drawers, or tallboy with brushing slide. The top half has a dentil frieze under the cornice and the sides are chamfered and reeded. The bracket feet are of ogee shape. The swan-neck handles are original. c.1760 - 70.

Price Range: £100 – £150

Value points: Size is not such an important factor, since most pieces are fairly large and for this reason not expensive. A height of six feet six inches or under would however add to value.

ref. **CH1438 (247)**

A late eighteenth century, c.1790, serpentine fronted mahogany low chest of drawers on splayed feet. There is an inlaid line of boxwood stringing around the top edge.

Price Range: £100 – £150

Value points: Size: Since this is a low chest, the width is not as critical a factor in the price as with normal chests, but still affects value.

ref. **CH1439 (245)**

A mahogany bow-fronted chest of drawers with brushing slide, c.1790. The four graduated drawers are cock-beaded. The splayed feet have a nicely shaped apron between them. The top is cross-banded with satin-wood, an unusual feature of quality.

Price Range: £185 – £225

Value points: Cross-banding of top ++

ref. **CH1440 (246)**
A late eighteenth century bow fronted mahogany chest of three drawers with brushing slide, splayed feet and attractive apron, c.1790.
Price Range: *£120 – £150*
Value points: *Low proportions +++*
Brushing slide ++

ref. **CH1441 (249)**

A bow fronted mahogany chest of drawers, c.1800, with ring handles and splayed feet.

Price Range: £60 – £90

Value points: Size: Height three feet six inches or under ++

ref. **CH1442 (250)**

A mahogany bow fronted chest of drawers, c.1800. This piece is of lower proportions, with deep drawers, and being thus somewhat smaller than the previous example, is in a slightly higher price range. The cockbeading around the drawer edges can be seen clearly.

Price Range: *£60 – £85*

Value points: See section notes

ref. **CH1443**

A mahogany clothes press or wardrobe, c.1800, showing the apron form and splay bracket feet typical of the Hepplewhite and Sheraton period. The top moulding is interesting in that it is a good example of an arcaded cavetto with a dentil course. The treatment of the doors on the wardrobe section is interesting in that it is one of mock drawer fronts the whole way down to watch the bottom chest section. Inset keyholes in ivory could be a later addition.

Price Range: £45 – £60

Value points: See section notes.

ref. **CH1444**

Military chests seem to have appeared some time after 1800 and were used by army officers up to the late 1870's. They were of course used for campaign purposes and were made in two halves which could be placed end to end to enable the owners to sleep on them. The flush-fitting drawer handles and brass-reinforced corners are a characteristic feature, as are the end carrying handles to each half. Usually they were made in mahogany but padouk, cedar and camphorwood examples are frequent. Sometimes the top drawer was fitted as a secretaire which adds greatly to value. There are still plenty of these chests about, but a great popularity amongst Americans and interior decorators, due to an appreciation of their undoubted merits of design, simplicity and durability in the modern home, has led to high prices compared to other chests of the period.

Iron carrying handles were frequently fitted originally as above, but nowadays fashion demands that they be replaced by elaborate brass ones of eighteenth century design.

Price Range: £85 – £110

Value points: rare exterior woods and drawer linings +++

ref. **CH1445**

A mahogany military chest of c.1845, fitted with a secretaire drawer. Although many such drawers provide only cramped writing space, the usefullness of them for selective storage and filing cannot be denied. The arrangement of small drawers and pigeon holes obviously varies from chest to chest and on rare occasions the entire long top drawer is fitted as a secretaire. Usually, as above, a small inset of tooled leather or baize covers the writing surface, as with bureaux.

Price Range: £110 – £150

Value points: The style of secretaire interior +++
  (Secret drawers add to value which also rises with the increasing number of small drawers)
  Rare exterior woods and drawer linings +++

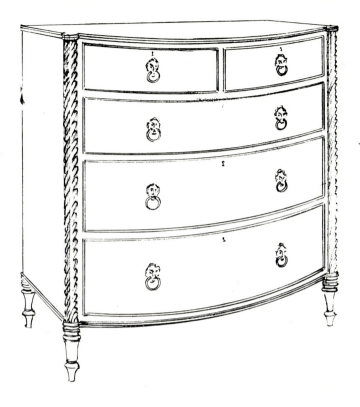

ref. **CH1446 (253)**

A Regency period mahogany bow-fronted chest of drawers, c.1830, with an applied solid twist or rope decoration down the front edge corners. The top and bottom edges are reeded. The turned legs give a hint of the rather bulbous turned examples that followed in the Victorian period. Although rather tall, the proportion of such chests is still good, particularly bearing in mind the larger houses which they were designed for.

Price Range: £90 – £120

Value points: Quality of wood used i.e. figure and decorative effect +++

ref. **CH1447 (254)**

Victorian mahogany bow-fronted chest of drawers on turned feet. The drawers have a heavy cock bead and the turned wooden knobs are also mahogany. The size of such chests tends to be large and cumbersome; the drawers less in number and hence deeper than earlier types, 1850 onwards.

Price Range: £10 – £20

Value points: Satinwood ++++
Figured veneers +++

ref. **CH1448**

A so-called 'Wellington' chest or more correctly, specimen cabinet, of c.1850. It is possibly due to the fact that the hinged side pieces or flaps lock over the drawers to prevent their opening during carriage and hence a possibly military or campaign advantage that the Wellington sobriquet has been given. Perhaps the largest concentration of drawers per foot super, obtainable in any piece of furniture is achieved by these chests, which are ideal for numismatists or specmien collectors. The taller types were often used for cutlery. Velvet lined drawers often indicate that the original purpose was in fact for collecting and some examples have grooved glass lids to the drawers. The example above is prettily veneered in walnut but rosewood, mahogany and maple were used as well as oak.

Price Range: £30 – £60

Value points: Decorative veneers +++
Specially fitted drawers +++
(Glass lids, compartments etc.).

ref. **CH1449 (255)**

A Victorian chest of drawers of c.1860. Usually made in mahogany. The ponderous moulded front of the top drawer throws the piece off balance and the bottom, with a solid flat base, raised slightly by turned knob feet, cannot hope to compensate in design. The turned wooden knobs are dear to the Victorian hearts and were frequently used as a replacement on chests of earlier periods in order to 'improve' them or bring them up to date — a vile practice which has ruined many fine eighteenth century pieces. Due to the fact that they are extremely solidly made, regrettably large numbers of these chests have survived.

Price Range: £7 – £12
Value points: None

BUREAUX

In the Middle Ages many small portable oak desks were made consisting of a simple box with sloping hinged lid on which the owner could write and keep his papers inside. Towards the end of the seventeenth century this form of desk also appears to have been made on a stand and our two first illustrations show clearly the desk form, overlapping the drawers added beneath and raised on legs which were either made in tapering or turned form. This type of bureau is also seen in the Queen Anne period raised on cabriole legs.

However, the usefulness of including drawer storage space beneath the desk could not be ignored, and the fall-front bureau with drawers beneath also appeared at the end of the seventeenth century. In some early examples the desk section also still overlaps the drawers beneath, but this soon gave way to the straight type, with perhaps a moulding under the desk section to mark the transition. Bureaux of this now conventional type continued to be made, first in walnut, then in mahogany, throughout the eighteenth century, many in country towns, and reflecting the changing styles of the period.

Bureau-Bookcases also appeared at the end of the seventeenth century and continued the same development, but with leanings towards bookcase styles. The increased height of rooms led to a demand for them. Early bookcases above bureaux either had solid doors or were glazed with Vauxhall glass mirrors, bevelled and, in the finer specimens, engraved.

Value points:

Early walnut bureaux on stands of the type illustrated in our first two examples have now become so rare that little can be said on the subject of value points except that the originality of the legs and stretchers is all-important and makes the difference between the prices shown and less than one half of them.

It should be noted that small bureaux, i.e. under 2' 9" wide, tend to have rather plain interiors, but the size criterion is the more important one, For bureaux generally, however, the following value points apply:-

Up to 1690 – Oak Period

    Structural condition and originality +++
    Colour and patination +++
    Original bun or bracket feet ++
    Size: Width 3' 0" or under ++
              Width 2' 9" or under +++
              Width 2' 6" or under ++++

Interior stepped +++
Well ++
Quality of mouldings ++
Original handles and keyhole plates ++

1680 – 1740 – The Walnut Period

1. Quality and figure of veneers, colour and patination +++
2. Structural condition and originality +++
3. Herringbone inlays and cross-banding ++
4. Stringing and other inlays ++
5. Marquetry ++++
6. Original brass handles and keyhole plates ++
7. Original bun or bracket feet ++
8. Colour (faded) and quality of crossgrained mouldings +++
9. Size: Width 3' 0" or under ++
   Width 2' 9" or under +++
   Width 2' 6" or under ++++
10. Interior stepped +++
11. Well ++
12. Oak drawer linings +

For oak and fruitwood examples of this period, value points 2, 4, 6, 7, 9, 10, 11 and 12 also apply with particular reference to size, plus the following:-

Choice of figured woods, colour and patination +++
Quality of mouldings ++

1730 onwards – The Mahogany Period

It should be remembered that mahogany and walnut periods over-lapped each other for about ten years from 1730-1740 and possibly longer. Value points for mahogany bureaux are:-

Quality and choice of figured wood, colour (faded or rich Spanish mahogany) and patination +++
Structural condition and originality +++
Original brass handles and keyhole plates ++
Size: Width 3' 0" or under ++
   Width 2' 9" or under +++
   Width 2' 6" or under ++++
Interior arrangement ++
Oak drawer linings + (Normal with good mahogany pieces)
Quality of mouldings ++
Original bracket feet +

For oak and fruitwood examples of the period the above points also apply.

ref. **B1500 (258)**

A William and Mary period, c.1690, walnut bureau of great quality. The tapering octagonal section solid walnut legs terminate in bun feet and the flat, shaped stretcher is also veneered in walnut. The arched shaping of the frieze with its small edge moulding, like a cock bead, is a fine example of the period. The fall front is cross-banded and has a herringbone inlay dividing it into three veneered panels with a cross-grained band between. The drawers are also herringbone cross-banded and there is a double 'D' moulding on the carcase edge around them. Note the book or bible-rest moulding on the bottom edge of the fall.

Price Range: £2,000 – £3,000

Value Points: Original legs and stretchers +++

ref. **B1501 (259)**

William and Mary walnut veneered walnut bureau with solid walnut octagonal tapering legs, c.1690. The X shaped stretcher is a feature found on tables of the period also, as are the bun feet. The fall front has a herringbone inlay and cross-banding. A half-round or D moulding covers the front edges of the carcase around the drawer fronts, which are herringbone cross-banded.

Price Range: £2,000 – £3,000

Value points: Original legs and stretchers +++

This is a delightfully small piece of furniture and hence its dimensions add greatly to its value.

ref. **B1502 (260)**

An oak bureau of c.1680, in which the union of the oak desk and a chest of drawers to make one piece of furniture is evident. A moulding still continues round the bottom of the desk section, even round the sides, and above the top drawer. The swan-neck handles are a later addition. The piece has the book or bible-rest moulding on the fall. The mouldings around the drawers and the division of the drawer fronts into panelled halves with a narrow raised centre panel is another contemporary feature which may be seen in the chest section of this book. The bun feet are also probably an original feature although, like the chests, some pieces had feet formed by the continuation of the carcase frame to the floor.

Price Range: £200 – £250

Value points: Quality of mouldings +++

ref. **B1503 (261)**

A walnut bureau of c.1690, the refined high quality version of the preceding example, made some years later. The style and origin are clear, even to the retention of the moulding around the base of the 'desk' section even though unnecessary structurally. The fall is divided into four beautifully matched sections of veneer, with a herringbone cross-banding and this effect is repeated on the drawer fronts. There is a double 'D' moulding on the carcase edges around the drawers. The heavy bracket feet are probably original but the handles and escutcheons are a later replacement.

Price Range: £500 – £700

Value points: Quality of decoration +++

ref. **B1504 (262)**

Another walnut bureau of William and Mary period, c.1700, this time open to show the stepped interior with fine concave drawer fronts. The pillars on either side of the centre drawer and pigeon hole can often be withdrawn as a 'secret' slender vertical drawer. There is a well in the centre interior reached by sliding the surface section in the centre back under the centre drawers. A cross-banded division on the side of the bureau is all that remains of the moulding dividing desk and drawers on the previous examples. The piece again exhibits herringbone cross-banding around the drawers and double 'D' moulding. The bracket feet, brass handles and escutcheons are probably original.

Price Range: £500 – £700

Value points: See section notes

ref. **B1505 (265)**

A Queen Anne, c.1710, walnut bureau bookcase of the slender 'single width' type with simple bookcase above. There is a bevelled edge period glass mirror in the door. The bureau section exhibits all the characteristics of ordinary bureaux of the period — herringbone inlays and cross-banding, drawer edge mouldings and stepped interior. The door on the bookcase is beautifully veneered in cross-banded effect.

Price Range: £3,000 – £4,000

Value points: See section notes

ref. **B1506 (266)**
A burr walnut bureau-bookcase of fine quality, c. 1720, with a broken pediment showing a fine bold cross-grained moulding. The bevelled door mirrors are edged by a thin 'D' moulding and beneath the doors the two tiny brass knobs indicate candle slides. The interior shows the pillar flanked door which has a star pattern inlay in boxwood and ebony. The exterior drawers are edged with cock-beading and have a herringbone inlay.

Price Range: £4,000 – £6,000

Value points: See section notes

ref. **B1507 (263)**

A William and Mary period fall-front secretaire cabinet on chest in walnut, c.1690. The heavy mouldings in cross-grained walnut, convex cushion drawer, and bun feet show the Dutch influence of William's reign. The piece is veneered in fairly straight grained English walnut without much figure and shows herringbone inlay around the panel in the fall as well as herringbone cross-banding on the drawers. The handles are of correct period style and may be original. Note that the veneer on the fall front is quartered, like chest tops of the period.

Price Range: £500 – £600

Value points: See section notes

ref. **B1508 (264)**

The walnut fall-front secretaire of the previous photograph shown open. Note the continuation of the drawer front style within, where herringbone corss-banding and simple half-round or 'D' mouldings echo the exterior arrangement. All the drawers in the piece are oak lined, even the convex fronted cushion drawer under the top moulding, which is a shallow drawer the full width of the piece. These fall front secretaires, although often finely made and exhibiting all the merits of their period decoratively, are not as popular as normal bureaux due to their size and lack of space under the fall when closed – we are all untidy with our papers and one cannot just drop them into the space under the fall on this piece, for it does not exist!

Price Range: *£500 – £600*

ref. **B1509 (268)**

A George I period walnut bureau-bookcase of heavier proportions, c.1720. The top of the bookcase shows the deep concave section, called a cavetto, below the moulding, veneered in crossgrained wood, which was a feature of later pieces of the walnut period. There are candle slides beneath the bookcase doors. The drawers have a lip edge moulding to overlap the flat veneered carcase edges.

Price Range: £2,000 – £2,500

Value points: See section notes

ref. **B1510 (267)**
A fine quality walnut Queen Anne period, c.1710, kneehole desk with top veneered in quartered pattern with herringbone inlays. The drawers are cross-banded and inlaid with herringbone pattern. The door inside the knee hole opens to give access to more smaller drawers.
Price Range: £800 – £1,200
Value points: See section notes

ref. **B1511 (269)**
Not a renegade from the chest section but a George I period secretaire tallboy in walnut veneer, c.1725. The top drawer front of the bottom chest falls forward to reveal secretaire fittings such as pigeon holes and small drawers for use as a writing piece. Otherwise the features are common to those of tallboys of the period, i.e. herringbone cross-banding, chamfered and fluted sides to the top half and a sunburst in the bottom drawers inlaid in boxwood and ebony.

Price Range: £350 – £500
Value points: See section notes

ref. **B1512 (270)**

A country bureau in solid walnut of c.1730. The interior shows the earlier William and Mary influence in the stepped concave drawers and well. The shaped aprons over the pigeon holes are also typical. The exterior drawers and outside of the fall are cross-banded in walnut or fruitwood. The handles are not original and the bracket feet have been repaired. The drawers are pine lined.

Price Range: £150 – £200

Value points: Quality of workmanship, i.e. approximation to contemporary town craftsmanship +++

ref. **B1513 (271)**

Country walnut (solid) bureau of c.1730, again showing William and Mary period influence in the stepped interior, but which is simpler and less refined than the previous example. The stepped drawers for instance are not concave. There is a well and the exterior drawers are again crossbanded in walnut or fruitwood.

Price Range: £125 – £175

Value points: See section notes

ref. **B1514 (272)**

A walnut bureau of c.1725-30, showing the interior, where the stepped design of the William and Mary period has given way to the Georgian straight interior with its corresponding loss of charm. The centre door is flanked by pillars with secret drawers. The interior and exterior drawers are inlaid with boxwood and ebony stringing. The carcase fronts around the drawers are flat veneered and the drawer edges have a 'lip' ovolo moulding. There is no interior well; a shallow drawer under the fall occupies this space.

Price Range: £400 – £500
Value points: See section notes

ref. **B1515**
An interesting mahogany bureau on stand, c.1740. The style is one which can be traced back to the Queen Anne period, when veneered walnut bureaux of this type, on stands with cabriole legs, were made. The early

ones incorporated the stylistic features of the period, with shell carving, quartered veneers and so on. The bureau above has cock-beaded drawers and swan-neck drop handles. The stand has rather provincial cabriole legs ending in pad or club feet and the flat facets at the knee have been left without brackets. A slight relic of former style is in the downward pointed centre apron, which would have been ogee curved or carved on earlier pieces.

The mahogany bureau, c.1740, of the preceding page, shown open. It can be seen that the interior also follows the style of an early period since it is stepped and the pigeon holes have arched shaping at the top, which incorporates the ogee curving of the Queen Anne period. There is no well and the drawer fronts are straight.

Price Range: £350 – £400

Value points: See preceding page

ref. **B1517 (274)**

An oak bureau of c.1740, with an unusual drawer arrangement in that there is a long drawer under the fall, thus ensuring that no interior well can be made, and subsequently the normal two short drawers and two long ones. The drawers have an ovolo lip moulding around the edge. The front surfaces of the piece are in fairly straight grained oak without the snaking medullary rays which tend to detract from the surface appearance of the wood. The simple bottom edge moulding and bold bracket feet are typical of country construction.

Price Range: *This is a smaller bureau – some 2' 9" wide – and therefore price would be affected. £175 – £225*

ref. **B1518 (275)**

Another oak bureau of c.1780, which provides an interesting comparison with the preceding example. The four long drawers are well graduated and have cock-beaded edges. The fall, however, is not made of one piece but is of a type often seen in mahogany construction, with a large centre section bounded by two edge pieces with vertical grain running at ninety degrees to the horizontal main section, and with mitre joints at the top corners*. The fall shows medullary rays in profusion. At the base the bracket feet are flush with the faces of the main carcase and a reeded moulding has been applied round the bottom edge.

Price Range: £140 – £180 (This is also 2' 9" wide)

Value points: See section notes

*Apart from a decorative effect, the purpose of this is in order to have edge mouldings running along the grain instead of across it.

ref. **B1519 (276)**

A mahogany kneehole desk of c.1750, with a broadly moulded top edge. The drawers have a lip moulding around the edge to project over the carcase edges when closed The bottom moulding above the bracket feet echoes the shape of the top edge, and the overall proportion is bold and pleasing.

Price Range: £400 – £600

Value points: See section notes
Brushing slide +++

ref. **B1520 (277)**

A mahogany bureau of c.1745 in a dark Spanish or Cuban variety of the wood which was the first type introduced. The later Honduras wood was lighter in weight and colour. The high bold bracket feet and simple proportions belie the much later ring handle replacements on the drawers. The original handles would have been much more in the style of the keyhole plates; in fact the escutcheons or back plates of the handles would have been almost exactly the same. Note the vertical grained veneering of the flat carcase fronts between the drawers and the plain vertically grained veneered sides.

Price Range: *£140 – £180*

Value points: *See section notes.*

ref. **B1521 (278)**

A typical mahogany bureau of the mid and later eighteenth century. The example illustrated here is perhaps a rather boldly wide one but as a type such bureaux, with cock-beaded drawers, were made in large numbers in a variety of sizes throughout the epoch. The mahogany varies in figure and decoration from piece to piece but they are extremely durable and many survive in almost original condition. At present, with walnut and oak making all the running, it could be that they are rather underpriced; the danger is that the larger ones tend to get converted into bureau-bookcases by the addition of a suitable cabinet. Size is, of course, an all-important factor in such pieces.

Price Range: £100 – £150
Value points: See section notes

ref. **B1522 (279)**

The mid-eighteenth century mahogany bureau of the previous example shown with the fall open. In this bureau the interior has not evolved greatly from earlier styles, being simple and straight fronted with shaped pigeon holes above the small drawers. The centre door is given a panelled effect and the overall style is bold and utilitarian as well as decorative. The centre interior well of the walnut styles has now completely disappeared and the top two short drawers slide immediately under the fall. The bracket feet are in solid mahogany with grain running horizontally as on the drawer fronts.

Price Range: *£100 – £150*

ref. **B1523 (280)**
An oak bureau of mid-eighteenth century date with the fall decorated by an inlaid star pattern in boxwood and ebony. This example is unusual in that the front edges are inset with a fluted pillar. The drawers are cock-beaded and their handles are not original, being in a later style. The original handles would have been in a shape more in keeping with the keyhole plates.

Price Range: £80 – £100
Value points: See section notes

ref. **B1524 (281)**
The mid-eighteenth century bureau of the preceding example shown with the fall open. The interior still owes much to earlier styles, with the outer pairs of drawers set forward from the line of the centre; they are not stepped vertically however. The inlaid star decoration and chequered panel line in boxwood and ebony on the centre door also owe their origin to earlier influences but the almost dentilled effect of the frieze under the top edge is of later inspiration. Note that the pillars of earlier designs on either side of the door have been replaced by a fluted surface.

Price Range: £80 - £100

ref. **B1525 (282)**

A mahogany bureau-bookcase of c.1750. The bureau section follows the characteristics of ordinary bureaux, with cock-beaded drawers, bracket feet and a straight interior under the fall, with no well. The bookcase section has mirrored doors and a dentil section incorporated in the top edge moulding. This is a simple and undecorated example of fairly broad dimensions.

Price Range: £300 – £500

Value points: See section notes

ref. **B1526 (285)**

A fine quality mahogany bureau-bookcase, c.1750, with broken pediment above and candle slides beneath the bookcase doors. The bureau section is made of well chosen figured mahogany and the piece appears to feature the unusual characteristics of having the two small upper drawers on either side beneath the fall to act as bearers for the fall when open. The shaping of the mirrored doors to echo the cornice, with its dentil frieze beneath the top moulding, adds considerable quality to the design.

Price Range: £500 – £700

Value points: See section notes

ref. **B1527 (283)**
A Chippendale mahogany kneehole desk of exceptional quality, c.1760. The front is of serpentine shape and the choice of veneers is extremely fine, showing pronounced figure. The mouldings show considerable refinement. A cock-bead is to be seen around the drawer edges and the shaping of the bracket feet is one typically attributed to the 'Chippendale' nomenclature.

Price Range: £1,000 – £1,200
Value points: Fretted edges +
　　　　　　　Pronounced mouldings +
　　　　　　　Bold sweep of front elevation ++

ref. **B1528 (284)**

A small George III period mahogany bureau on ogee bracket feet, c.1770 This is a veneered piece, evidently because the wood is so finely figured and would have been wasteful to use in the solid. There is a chequered stringing line around each cock-beaded drawer and the fall, which are cross-banded. The inside is fitted with pigeon holes and five drawers.

Price Range: £250 – £300

Value points: Ogee bracket feet ++

ref. **B1529 (288)**

A bureau-bookcase of the Hepplewhite period c.1790, in which the change to the latticed glazed doors instead of mirrors, which took place after the mid-eighteenth century, is demonstrated. A broken arched pediment with pierced fret completes the design above a dentillated moulding. The bureau section reflects the change towards commodes in the chest of drawers field, in that panelled veneered doors enclose the drawers below the fall. The feet are still of bracket type but a shaped apron between them reflects the taste of the last part of the eighteenth century.

Price Range: £2,000 – £2,500

Value points: This is an extremely fine example as far as choice of veneers and craftsmanship are concerned, hence the high price scale.

See section notes.

ref. **B1530 (289)**

A mahogany secretaire-bookcase of c.1790 reflecting more of the Sheraton nomenclature in its squarer lines. The latticed glazed doors and simple top moulding reflect a more refined style. The top drawer of the chest section falls to reveal a secretaire. The feet are of the tapering, slightly splayed type with curved apron attributed to Hepplewhite/Sheraton but probably more simply in the then current taste.

Price Range: £500 – £600

Value points: See section notes

                Satinwood ++++

ref. **B1531 (287)**
An early nineteenth century mahogany bureau with symmetrical veneers in a vertical grained figure, c.1820. The interior is straight, with pigeon holes and drawers and the sides are of solid mahogany. In the later period the veneered pieces tended to be of better quality, usually lined in oak.
Price Range: £90 – £120
Value points: See section notes

ref. **B1532 (290)**

A Georgian partner's desk with red tooled leather inset on the top, c.1790. These mahogany partner's desks continued to be made for a considerable period and have been reproduced for many years. The construction of the drawers with cock-beaded edges, and the top edge mouldings, are in the same style as the other pieces of the period, generally following the library tables of the end of the century.

Price Range: £350 – £500

Value points: See section notes

ref. **B1533 (291)**
An early nineteenth century mahogany bureau on splayed feet with a shaped apron, c.1820. The fall is cross-banded and the drawers have a normal cock-bead. Due to the angle of the photograph the bureau appears to be perched rather high on its legs, but its proportion follows that of the chests of drawers of the same period.

Price Range: £80 – £100
Value points: See section notes

ref. **B1534 (292)**

A 'Carlton House' writing table so much associated with the Regency period. A table of this type was illustrated in Hepplewhite's second edition of *'The Cabinet Maker's Book of Prices'* but the name was first found in Gillows Cost Books for 1796. Sheraton described the plate as a Lady's Drawing or Writing Table and states that it is to be made in satinwood or mahogany with a brass rim round the top part.

Price Range: £2,000 *upwards*
Value points: Quality of decoration +++
                    Satinwood ++

N.B. Writing tables of this type were made on throughout the nineteenth century and one of these reproductions was sold recently for £230 at auction in London.

ref. **B1535 (293)**

A Davenport veneered in satinwood of c.1800. The name of this piece of furniture is assumed to have arisen from Gillows Cost Books in the late eighteenth century, where the entry 'Captain Davenport, a desk' occurs. The sloping lid and brass gallery are characteristic and this example has a slide above the drawers on the right hand side. There is a set of false drawer fronts down the left hand side not seen in this photograph. The lid is inset with tooled leather.

Price Range: £150 – £200
Value points: Satinwood +++
Regency Period +++

ref. **B1536 (294)**

A later Regency period mahogany Davenport, c.1830, with interesting turned columns. The lid is inset with leather and the top or desk section exhibits the same small drawer let into the right hand side as in the previous example. It has been suggested that this was a useful way to keep ink away from the documents inside the piece. The drawers on the right hand side are the opening ones; a set of false drawer fronts decorates the left side, unseen in this photograph.

Price Range: £60 – £90

Value points: Regency period +++
Decorative veneers +++

ref. **B1537 (295)**
A Victorian burr walnut Davenport of c.1850. The top section can be released by a catch under the lid to pop up on a spring and is fitted with pigeon holes. The serpentine shaped front and cabriole fashion front supports are typical of the better quality Victorian versions of this piece of furniture. The lid is inset with red tooled leather.

Price Range: £60 – £80
Value points: Burr walnut +++
              Decoration ++

ref. **B1538 (296)**
Regency period satinwood secretaire with turned and fluted tapering legs, c.1830. There is a brass gallery rail around the top edge above the external pigeon holes. The fall-front encloses further pigeon holes and drawers.
Price Range: £120 – £180
Value points: Satinwood +++

ref. **B1539**

A Victorian period pedestal desk of c.1840 with leather top. This example is on casters but many stood simply on the aproned base. These desks were made in very large quantities throughout the nineteenth century for an enormously increasing market in office and home. Mahogany and oak were probably the most frequently employed woods but pine, rosewood, walnut and other woods were also used. There are veneered examples in walnut, mahogany, rosewood and maple. Most of them are made to fit against a wall, but the 'partner's' variety i.e. made to be free-standing with cupboards or panelled fronts, are the more valuable.

Price Range: *'Partner's' type £80 – £160*
                   Other £60 – £100
Value points: *Antique leather top ++*
                   Decorative woods +++
                   Original lock (and key) +

ref. **B1540**

An Edwardian inlaid bureau with cylinder front, c.1905. Eighteenth century and Regency styles became popular at the end of the nineteenth century and this is a good example of Edwardian 'Sheraton'. The square tapering legs with their thin stringing line end in casters. The inlay of the rosewood drawers and front is however, more profuse, and incorporates Adam motifs, whereas the gallery shows Gothic arching. Beneath the cylinder front, itself a feature of the late eighteenth century, there is a slide which pulls out to provide additional writing space. Highly exportable.

Price Range: *£60 – £80*

Value points: Decorative woods and inlays +++

DRESSERS

The demarcation between cupboards and dressers in the seventeenth century is somewhat difficult to define, particularly where the lower portion is enclosed by doors. About 1650 and afterwards, it was common to have dressers which were without the upper super-structure although sometimes shelves may have been fastened to the wall above. Naturally, these dressers reflected the style of the period as far as drawer decoration and leg turning was concerned. In country districts dressers were made by local craftsmen on throughout the eighteenth century long after they had ceased to be fashionable in town houses. In this way the cabriole leg continued to appear on dressers when it had disappeared on other town-made furniture. In the second half of the eighteenth century side cupboards were included in the upper half and the top cornice carried mouldings copied from more refined furniture, such as dentil friezes. The dresser does not appear to have developed much beyond this period, since it has long been relegated to a piece of kitchen furniture it may have been neglected stylistically for this reason.

The prices given are assuming good structural condition and originality.

Pine Dressers

The undoubted lightness of colour and prevalent vogue for stripped pine has led to a spectacular rise in price for these pieces. In general, pine dressers appeared much later than oak or elm ones and are mostly nineteenth century. Many were made in the form of a built-in unit designed to be pinned to a kitchen wall and were painted. The increased availability of caustic tanks has made stripping easier and their rather naked and loose-jointed appearance was not an original intention. Some are undoubtedly very pretty and the country ones are sturdy. They are extremely useful and are often used to show off pretty patterned plates which would otherwise have been quite rightly smashed as junk.

Price Range: £60 – £150
Value points: Ogee curved shaped aproning or frieze +++
*   Spice drawers +++*
*   Galleries or special cupboards +++*

ref. **D1600 (300)**

A fine Charles II period small oak dresser, c.1670. The drawers illustrate the geometrical mouldings found on chests of the period — the swan-neck handles are a replacement and simple pear-drops or pulls would have been more likely. The legs show a fine example of Restoration turning with inverted cup and baluster forms. Although the legs finish square in section as though to take stretchers, these were not originally fitted. The top edge surface shows a simple thumb nail moulding and the cornice beneath shows a fine bold concave form.

Price Range: £500 – £600

Value points: Small Size – five feet to six feet long +++
Quality of leg turning +++
Drawer mouldings +++
Colour and patination +++
Original handles ++

ref. **D1601 (301)**

Another fine larger oak dresser of c.1680. The drawers show the same form as the previous example, with mitred decorative mouldings, but applied split baluster forms decorate the frame at the sides and between them. The legs show fine column turning of the same form as our gate-leg table illustrated in that section. Again the legs are squared above the turned feet as though to take stretcher joints, but in fact stretchers are only fitted at the side.

Price Range: £400 – £500

Value points: Size – length six feet or under ++++
Colour and patination +++
Quality of drawer mouldings +++
Quality of leg turning +++
Original handles ++

ref. **D1602 (302)**

A fruitwood dresser of c.1720 date. The drawers show a simpler form of the earlier moulded panels but the top edge mouldings retain the same form. The cupboard door panels are also moulded with mock drawer fronts in the top half to retain proportion.

Price Range: £280 – £325

Value points: Fruitwood +++
　　　　　　　Colour and patination +++
　　　　　　　Quality of mouldings +++
　　　　　　　Original handles ++

ref. **D1603 (303)**

A rather more countrified dresser of c.1720, showing very simple leg turning. The shaped apron with projecting lip moulding follows that of side table styles of the period. The drawer fronts are very simple but there is a form of cock-bead around them on the frame. The top edge has a simple thumb-nail moulding.

Price Range: £140 – £160

Value points: Size – seven feet wide or under +++
Colour and patination +++
Quality of mouldings ++
Original handles ++

ref. **D1604 (304)**

An oak dresser of c.1725 with upper shelves. The top cornice has an ogee moulding and shaped frieze beneath. The door panels are fielded and shaped, with the solid panel between them repeating this form. The drawers are simple, with no moulding, but the frame around them and the cupboard doors show a simple moulded edge. Note the panelled side to the lower section.

Price Range: £300 – £350

Value points: Small Size +++
　　　　　　　Colour and patination +++
　　　　　　　Fielded door panels ++
　　　　　　　Original handles ++
　　　　　　　Quality of mouldings ++

ref. **D1605 (305)**

An oak dresser of c.1725 also, but without the upper structure. The cupboard doors are again fielded and shaped. There is also the same moulded edge form on the frame around doors and drawers. The latter are simple; the handles are not original. Note that the sides are panelled; a form found on chests of drawers of the previous century.

Price Range: *£150 – £200*
Value points: *Small Size +++*
                Colour and patination +++
                Quality of mouldings ++
                Original handles ++

ref. **D1606 (306)**

A much simpler and cruder oak dresser of c.1730, with simple single cupboard door. There is a simple thumb-nail moulding round the top edge and the frame also has a simple moulding around drawers and panel edges.

Price Range: £100 – £150

Value points: Small Size +++
Colour and patination +++
Quality of mouldings ++
Original handles ++

ref. **D1607 (307)**

An oak dresser of c.1750 period on cabriole legs. The upper part is fitted with three spice drawers, which adds to value. The top edge moulding is rather more sophisticated and the drawers have an ovolo lip moulding around the edge to lap over the carcase frame. The cabriole legs are well shaped ending in a pad foot.

Price Range: £250 – £300

Value points: Small Size +++
　　　　　　　Colour and patination +++
　　　　　　　Spice drawers +++
　　　　　　　Cabriole legs +++
　　　　　　　Original handles ++

ref. **D1608 (308)**

An oak dresser of c.1750. The top cornice shows a dentillated section in the moulding with a shaped frieze beneath. The side cupboard doors are panelled and moulded. The drawers are cock-beaded and the swan-neck handles are possibly original. The shaped apron repeats the curves of the top frieze. It is interesting to note the C scroll behind the knee on the cabriole legs — a sign of quality coming from cabrioles of the Queen Anne period.

Price Range: £300 – £400
Value points: Small Size +++
Cabriole legs +++
Colour and patination +++
Quality of mouldings ++
Shaped apron and frieze +++

ref. **D1609 (309)**

A cupboarded oak dresser of c.1760, with fielded panels in doors and drawers. The cupboards on either side of the upper structure have a spice drawer beneath. The whole form of construction dates from a much earlier period, showing how country craftsmen retained these methods long after they were superseded elsewhere.

Price Range: £200 – £250

Value points: Small Size ++++
Colour and patination +++
Spice drawers ++
Original handles ++

ref. **D1610 (310)**

A later eighteenth century oak dresser, of c.1790, with drawers crossbanded in mahogany. The top cornice is well moulded and the row of spice drawers in the upper section adds greatly to value. The crossbanded drawers are cock-beaded and it can be seen that small drawers have been let into the frieze. The 'gallery' beneath with its useful floor-level shelf was used for larger kitchen utensils and pots.

Price Range: *£200 – £300*
Value points: *Small Size ++++*
              Colour and patination +++
              Spice drawers +++
              Original handles ++
              Quality of leg turning ++

ref. **D1612 (311)**

A Welsh oak dresser of last quarter of the eighteenth century. Note that the drawers are cock-beaded and that the shaped central apron reflects a form of much earlier origin. The apron is also cock-beaded like some Queen Anne forms. The panelled or boarded-in back gives a heavier appearance and it is well to remember that many may have had this removed.

Price Range: £150 – £200

Value points: Small size ++++
Colour and patination +++
Original handles ++
Quality of leg turning ++

ref. **D1613 (297)**

An oak Court cupboard — no not a buffet — of the early seventeenth century. The shelves at the front are supported by the typical bulbous carved form seen on refectory tables of the period. At the back the flat supports are fluted on the front surface. Variations to be found include human and animal forms such as gryphons acting as front supports. Some pieces show very fine examples of rich carving but on the whole this is not a popular piece of furniture considering its antiquity, due to the modern avoidance of heavy forms.

Price Range: *£150 – £200*

Value points: *Quality of carving +++ or even ++++*
                 Colour and patination +++

ref. **D1614 (298)**

An oak hall cupboard probably of the late seventeenth or early eighteenth century. A piece of furniture used in halls and living rooms of the seventeenth century which was made on into the eighteenth century by country craftsmen. In the early forms the turned pendants, which appeared in Cromwellian times, were replaced by the turned bulbous pilasters seen on court cupboards and tables of the first half of the seventeenth century. Baluster forms continued to appear however, as well as turned pendants, until the end of the century. In Wales similar pieces were made on into the mid-eighteenth century but in England they were gradually superseded from the beginning of the eighteenth century by the farmhouse dresser.

Price Range: £125 – £150
Value points: Rich carving and inlays ++++
*   Colour and patination +++*

SIDEBOARDS AND CHIFFONIERS

The sideboard proper, as distinct from the side or sideboard table, is an eighteenth century innovation generally attributed to Adam, who had the idea of grouping a sideboard table with an urn-mounted pedestal at each end, around 1760. Before that, one can trace through the sixteenth and seventeenth century the various forms of side table for dining use including court cupboards and dressers, but these had been somewhat out of fashion among the wealthy from the beginning of the eighteenth century. In the Adam arrangement, the centre table had a brass gallery at the back or top for supporting plates and the urns on each pedestal were used, one for iced water for drinking, the other for hot water for washing the silver. The pedestals were used as a plate warmer and cellaret respectively. Later in the century, the arrangement became less massive and the pedestals were omitted, with drawer space in the table taking their place. This later development led to the later Georgian sideboards we associate with the name. Shearer and Hepplewhite illustrated the type with pedestals and so did Sheraton, but Gillows appears to have produced the type with lateral drawers in the last quarter of the eighteenth century. In the Regency period the side drawers were extended to form cupboards reaching the floor and proportions again became massive. Sideboards suffered the same fate as other Regency furniture in the form of zoological embellishment in an attempt to design on classical and Oriental lines.

In the same period, the chiffonier was originated as a separate form, with shelves above and cupboards below. The doors of the cupboard were often latticed in brass with silk backing. During the Victorian period the chiffonier and the sideboard appear to have become inextricably entwined and it is difficult to separate them terminologically.

For the sideboards illustrated, we have assumed that condition structurally and originality are good. Otherwise, the following common value points apply:-

>Colour and patination +++
>Figured woods and decoration +++
>Width under five feet ++
>Width under four feet +++
>Tambour shutter +

For chiffoniers:-

>Brass lattice ++
>Rosewood +

ref. **S1700 (313)**
A mahogany sideboard with tambour snutter below the centre drawer, c.1780. The top and the drawers are cross-banded in satinwood and the oval panel in each deep side drawer is banded with a satinwood inlay also. The mahogany veneers used are highly figured. Width six feet.

Price Range: *£400 – £600*
Value points: Satinwood cross-banding +++

ref. **S1701 (314)**
A magnificently decorated mahogany sideboard with broken serpentine front, c.1790. One of the two deep drawers is in fact a cupboard. The six square tapering legs are on spade feet. The top is cross-banded in tulipwood and has a satinwood oval with a shell. The front drawers are all cross-banded with tulipwood and inlaid with satinwood corners and satinwood spandrels. Five feet seven inches wide.

Price Range: £600 – £800
Value points: Decoration +++

ref. **S1702 (315)**
A mahogany serpentine front sideboard, the top cross-banded with satinwood, of c.1790. Again an oval panel decorates the deep drawers and the arched brackets under the centre drawer are inlaid with a fan or shell motif in satinwood. The six square tapering legs are inlaid with satinwood in classical style obviously of Adam influence. The width of this particular example is only four feet four inches hence the higher price scale.

Price Range: £600 – £750
Value points: Inlaid decoration +++

ref. **S1703 (316)**

A later Georgian serpentine mahogany sideboard of c.1795. In this case there is no satinwood banding or inlay and the four square tapering legs are somewhat more substantial in order to sustain the weight. Width four feet eight inches.

Price Range: £350 – £450

Value points: See section notes

ref. **S1704 (317)**
An unusual Regency period sideboard in walnut of c.1820 where a return to the classical design is evident in the pedestals, which are fitted as a wine cooler and storage space for napery. The reeded columns and paw feet, as well as the lion masks are very characteristic of Regency styles.
Price Range: £150 – £200
Value points: See section notes

ref. **S1705 (318)**

A mahogany sideboard of c.1810 on four turned legs and without any shaped arching of the centre space. The shape reiterates more simply the earlier forms but the turning on the legs shows signs of later overdeveloped design.

Price Range: £100 – £150
Value points: See section notes

ref. **S1706 (319)**
A Regency mahogany chiffonier or cabinet, c.1825, with reeded shelves above and cross-banded doors with brass lattices backed by pleated silk. A simple and restrained example of a piece of furniture which originated as an incidental cupboard or commode.

Price Range: £125 – £150

Value points: See section notes

ref. **S1707 (320)**

A Regency mahogany chiffonier, c.1825, with a brass gallery around the upper shelf. The two supporting columns are also brass. This is a slightly later example where the style has become a little less restrained in the curving sides and feet. The brass lattices in the doors are again backed by pleated silk.

Price Range: £100 – £130

Value points: See section notes

N.B. It is again useful to note that this piece of furniture could be described as a cabinet or commode and probably originated as a piece of lady's incidental furniture.

ref. **S1708 (321)**
A Regency chiffonier, c.1825, of rather more ornate type, often found in rosewood. The shelves have mirror backs and are supported by curved brackets in receding proportion. The sides are reeded and the doors latticed.

Price Range: £120 – £150
Value points: See section notes

ref. **S1709 (322)**
A Victorian mahogany chiffonier, c.1840, in well-figured wood with a drawer fitted flush under the top. There is another, floor level drawer under the solid, cross-banded cupboard doors. A pleasantly simple design.
Price Range: £40 – £60
Value points: See section notes

ref. **S1710 (323)**

A later Victorian chiffonier, c.1860, in carved mahogany with mirror back and glazed side doors. Electro-gilt metal mounts on such pieces replace the restrained brass of the Regency. Marble-topped versions without the mirror back but with mirrored doors are still common.

Price Range: £40 – £60

Value Points: Size – many of these pieces are far too large for the modern house. A ++++ factor can therefore be assumed for small, manageable examples.

CORNER CUPBOARDS

Although corner cupboards were made throughout the seventeenth century they do not seem to have come into more general use until the end of it. From then until about 1750, corner cupboards were made in the prevailing taste for town use, but subsequently they seem to have retired to the country as far as manufacture is concerned. For this reason perhaps, the majority of hanging corner cupboards found in shops nowadays are of later eighteenth century date and often made of oak, with mahogany cross-banding or decoration. Inlaid shells and paterae are also frequently found in these later pieces.

It is almost certain that bow-fronted corner cupboards fetch more in price than flat ones; generally due to their greater elegance, as a general form, however, the corner cupboard is not over-popular and has not appreciated in value as much as more utilitarian pieces in the everyday sense such as chairs, chests, dining tables and bureaux. The pine open corner cupboards of Essex type have had something of a vogue and can generally be put to more decorative use than the closed hanging type.

ref. **CC1750 (325)**

A walnut cross-banded glazed-door corner cupboard of c.1725, with broken pediment. It has been suggested that such cupboards became popular at the time to store and display the expensive tea sets then in vogue. The figure of the walnut veneers is elegantly matched and the moulding on the cornice is gross-grained.

Price Range: £250 – £350

Value points: Quality of decoration and veneers +++
               Quality of colour and cross-grained mouldings +++
               Quality of glazing ++

ref. **CC1751 (326)**
A walnut bow-fronted corner cupboard with cross-banding, c.1720. Possibly designed to stand on a larger bow-fronted corner cupboard.
Price Range: £100 – £150
Value Points: Small size +++
                Quality, figure and patination of veneer ++

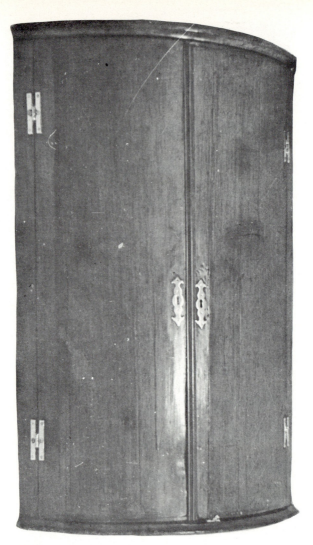

ref. **CC1752 (327)**
Solid walnut bow-fronted corner cupboard of c.1730, of country origin. The construction and mouldings are very simple.

Price Range: £60 – £90

Value points: Colour and patination +++
                 Size – small ++
                 Quality of mouldings ++

ref. **CC1753 (328)**

An oak corner cupboard of c.1740, with panelled doors banded in mahogany. Cupboards of this style, often as a low stand were made from the beginning of the century onwards but the dentillated top cornice and mahogany decoration indicate the date mentioned. Rather a large form of corner cupboard generally.

Price Range: £70 – £90

Value Points: Colour and patination +++
Quality of mouldings ++

ref. **CC1755 (329)**

A mid eighteenth century oak bow-fronted corner cupboard with fluted pilasters. The 'H' hinges are typical of the type used by country makers, although the pilasters add quality to the piece, c.1750.

Price Range: £60 – £70

Value Points: Colour and patination +++
Small size ++

ref. **CC1754 (330)**

Mid eighteenth century mahogany corner cupboard, c.1750, with broken pediment and panelled doors. The moulding to the cornice is finely executed and the dark figured mahogany in the shaped door panels is rich in colour.

Price Range: £60 – £80

Value points: Size – slender width +++
Colour and patination +++
Figure of wood and decoration +++
Moulded cornice ++

ref. **CC1756 (332)**
Oak bow-fronted country corner cupboard with mahogany banding on the doors. Probably of late eighteenth century date. The top moulding is dentillated and there is an inlaid medallion in boxwood and ebony at the top of the flat side surfaces, c.1780.

Price Range: £35 – £50

Value points: Colour and patination +++
  Size – slender in width ++
  Decorations and inlays ++

ref. **CC1757** (̄334)

A late eighteenth century oak corner cupboard with a panelled door with three drawers below. Beneath the bold top cornice moulding there is a band of mahogany veneer. The three small drawers suggest that the piece may have been designed for kitchen use although the quality of construction and door panel moulding are of fairly refined craftsmanship. c.1790.

Price Range: £40 – £50

Value Points: *Colour and patination +++*
　　　　　　　　Decoration and inlays +++
　　　　　　　　Quality of mouldings ++
　　　　　　　　Drawers below +

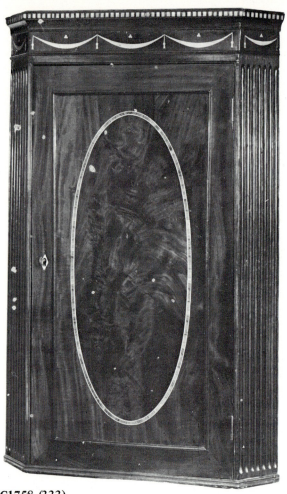

ref. **CC1758 (333)**

Late eighteenth century mahogany corner cupboard with fluted sides and decorated with satinwood inlays. The oval central panel to the door is decorated with a beautifully figured piece of mahogany veneer. The top cornice is dentillated with satinwood inlay and the frieze is also decorated with an inlaid satinwood classical motif, c.1790.

Price Range: £45 – £65

Value points: Colour and patination +++
Figure of wood and decoration +++
Size – slender width ++

NIGHT TABLES

In the second half of the eighteenth century a form of cupboard on legs became very popular as a night table or commode to hold a chamber pot. It is known that Chippendale supplied this type of article and that Ince and Mayhew as well as Sheraton, illustrated various designs of this type of furniture. Some types are designed to look like a small chest of drawers, but the top is hinged at the back to act as a lid to lift up and stand perpendicularly. There were examples which were quite ornate, being, in the later years of the century, veneered in satinwood and subject to decoration in the prevailing styles. Even small convertable sets of steps were made for the purpose. In recent years they have again become popular as occasional tables for bedside use or even for containing gramaphone equipment.

ref. **NT1770 (336)**
A mahogany night table with fretted tray handles to the top edge, c.1780. The front has a lifting shutter and the shaped apron beneath is the front of the pot holding drawer; it draws forward with the legs, which are split across the section.

Price Range: £60 – £80

Value Points: Tray top ++
                Colour and patination +++
                Figured woods and veneers +++

ref. **NT1771 (337)**

A mahogany night table of c.1790, with cupboard panelled doors and 'tray' top. The complete front lower section is attached to the front of the pot drawer and all slides forward. The front legs are split diagonally so that adequate support is obtained when the drawer is open.

Price Range: *£50 – £60*

Value points: *Colour and patination +++*
Figured woods and inlays +++
Tray top ++

ref. **NT1772 (338)**

A good quality mahogany night table with tambour shutter which slides horizontally across the front, and 'tray' top, with handles fretted into the rim. The tambour shutter, when opened, slides round the inside edge of the cupboard space. The pot holding drawer front has been simulated to look like two cock-beaded and veneered drawers. The front legs are again split so that support is given to the drawer front when open, c.1790.

Price Range: £60 – £80

Value points: Tambour shutter +++
                 Colour and patination +++
                 Figured woods and inlays +++
                 Tray top ++

ref. **NT1773 (339)**
A smaller mahogany night table with tambour shutter and tray top. The pot drawer is similar to the previous examples with split front leg and a simple turned wooden knob, c.1800.

Price Range: *£50 – £70*

Value points: *Tambour shutter +++*
Colour and patination +++
Figured woods and inlays +++
Tray top ++

ref. **NT1774**

A circular Victorian night table with marble top of c.1855. These pieces are usually made of mahogany and represent something of an achievement in veneering on a curved surface and in steaming. Inside they are predictably simple.

Price Range: £15 – £25
Value points: Figured woods +++
Inlays ++

ref. **NT1775**

A **Victorian** night table of c.1870. Made in mahogany or veneered in walnut, these cabinets have yet to find their collectors. They must have been produced for many years and do not represent any particular achievement of construction.

Price Range: 10/- up to whatever can be successfully conned out of you.
Value points: None

WORK TABLES

Work tables for use by ladies, with space for needlework materials in a well below were a later eighteenth century phenomenon and were made in a variety of forms. We have illustrated some typical examples and have included a number without the silk bag but with small drawers instead. It can be mentioned that Sheraton illustrated some designs, as did Gillows. In the Regency period and after, some very elaborately decorated designs appeared in a variety of styles; the later Victorian type of octagonal form, with tapering well, supported on a tripod base, have recently become popular and are being sold in a range from £15 – £25 depending on the veneered surface decoration.

ref. **WT 1780 (340)**

A Regency work table in burr walnut with side drop flaps and three drawers, on Disneyesque paw feet with reeded scrolls. Under the lowest drawer a slide acts as a drawer frame for the pleated silk bag, c.1825.

Price Range: £80 – £100

Value points: Burr Walnut +++

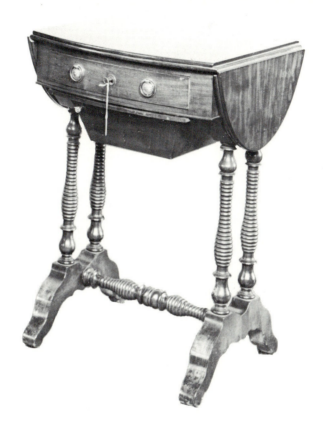

ref. **WT1781 (341)**

A Regency mahogany work table with drop flaps and a centre drawer with work bag sliding beneath. The end supports consist of two turned columns on raised feet and a turned stretcher, in the same style, c.1815.

Price Range: *£80 – £100*

Value points: Figured woods and inlays +++
               Quality of turning +++

ref. **WT1782 (342)**
A Regency yew wood work table on a turned baluster stem and four carved feet ending in brass paw casters, c.1820. An unusually circular piece, which, had it been in any other wood than yew, should not have been priced at more than £50.

Price Range: £120 – £170
Value points: Figure and inlays +++

ref. **WT1783 (343)**

An early Victorian mahogany work table with folding top, two drawers and silk bag on slide. Supported on an octagonal centre column on shaped platform on turned flat bun feet, c.1840.

Price Range: £50 – £70

Value points: Figured woods and inlays +++

ref. **WT1784 (353)**

A late Georgian mahogany work table with three shallow drawers, inlaid with boxwood stringing. Note here again the slightly 'bamboo' effect in the turning of the tapering legs, c.1800.

Price Range: £70 – £90

Value points: Choice of figured woods and inlays +++
                  Quality of leg turning +++

ref. **WT1785 (354)**

A simple mahogany work table of c.1845 date. The turned legs are simply executed and the mahogany is not greatly figured. The casters are original.

Price Range: £45 – £65

Value points: Figured woods and inlays +++
Quality of leg turning ++

ref. **WT1786 (355)**

A Regency period work table on tripod stand, in mahogany. There are two flaps, Pembroke table style, which can be supported on brackets, to give greater surface area to the top. The two drawers open at the visible end; on the other end two mock drawer surfaces are included to give balance, c. 1815.

Price Range: £100 – £140

Value points: Elegance of tripod stand +++
Choice of figured woods and inlays +++

ref. **WT1787 (356)**

A Regency work table in mahogany with three drawers veneered in figured wood. The centre column is turned and carved with leaf pattern. The four carved legs end in paw feet on casters. Note that the drawer fronts are cross-banded, c.1830.

Price Range:
Price Range: *£100 – £150*
Value points: Figured woods and inlays +++
                        Quality of base +++

ref. **WT1788**

A japanned and painted work table of c.1840. It is constructed on the Pembroke table principle with two side flaps which are supported by small hinged wooded brackets. The drawers are cock-beaded.

Price Range: *£60 – £80*
Value points: *Quality of painted decoration +++*
                 Mother of pearl inlays ++

ref. **WT1789**

A Victorian walnut work table of c.1860 date. The octagonal top lifts to give access to a compartmented interior and the tapering central column is hollow to allow for storage of wools. It is raised on carved cabriole legs. Usually the tops of such pieces are veneered with a thin sheet of decorative burr, but mahogany and rosewood examples with variations exist Marquetry inlaid tops are also fairly common in the walnut varieties.

Price Range: **£**25 – £30

    points: Inlays +++
        Silk lined interior +++
        Decorative veneered top +++

N.B. The lids usually made of cheap pine on to which the mahogany was veneered, often warped and, therefore, do not close properly.

CANTERBURIES

The most common form of Canterbury now found in antique shops is in fact the music Canterbury, which is illustrated in the pages which follow. However, there were supper Canterburies (one illustrated by Sheraton) and atlas Canterburies. It seems that the name comes from an Archbishop of that See who liked his furniture mobile and convenient. The supper Canterbury was in fact a forerunner of the modern tea-trolley, being equipped with cutlery and plates. However, these are now rare and, by Canterbury, it is now generally accepted that the term is used to describe the music variety. They are very convenient for holding newspapers and magazines but at present seem to be considerably overpriced in relation to other furniture.

ref. **CA1800 (344)**

A late Georgian 'Canterbury' music stand of the type described in Sheraton's *'Cabinet Dictionary'* of 1803. Note the turned legs and uprights but flat mahogany divisions. The drawer below is veneered in figured mahogany and the central division is fretted to provide a carrying handle.

Price Range: £150 – £200

Value points: Exotic woods +++

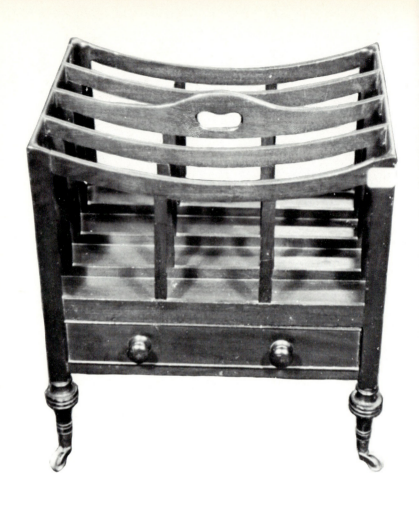

ref. **CA1801 (345)**

A mahogany 'Canterbury' music stand of the type described in Sheraton's *'Cabinet Dictionary'* of 1803. These later Georgian pieces were designed to hold music and later papers of other descriptions. Note the turned legs on casters and the flat mahogany divisions. Later Victorian examples tended to have turned divisions. The centred one in this case is fretted to provide a carrying handle.

Price Range: £150 – £200

Value points: Rosewood or other exotic woods +++

ref. **CA1802**
A rosewood Canterbury of c.1840 with turned outer supports and legs. There are both turned and flat dividing supports, however. The concave box section beneath contains a drawer.
Price Range: £50 – £70

ref. **CA1803 (346)**

A mid-Victorian, c.1860, mahogany carved music Canterbury and stand. The rather delicately carved top gallery rail and twist turned vertical columns lend considerable quality to the piece.

Price Range: £40 – £60

ref. **TP1810 (347)**

A Regency period rosewood teapoy, c.1820, on baluster-turned stem with tripod base, the feet ending in brass paw casters. More and less elaborate examples exist, continuing into the Victorian period. The interior is divided into three sections with rosewood lids, each section having a metallic lining.

Price Range: £60 – £80
Value points: Rosewood ++
  Inlaid decoration +++
  Original cut-glass fittings +++

ref. **TP1811**

A rosewood teapoy of c.1840 on a tapering column. The top is of simple design relieved by a small bead mould around the edge of the lid. Like the tea and tripod tables of the period, the base has become a flat plinth, shaped in cusped curves and standing on turned knob feet.

Price Range: £30 – £50

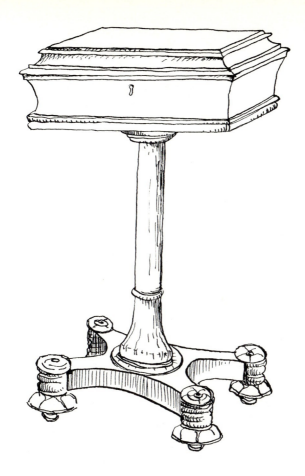

ref. **TP1812 (348)**

A Victorian rosewood teapoy, c.1850. The base, with its pillar support on a shaped flat platform with turned feet is typical of the Victorian designs which can be seen on later tables which replaced the tripod. The interior is divided into compartments like the preceding Regency example.

Price Range: £30 – £50

Value points: Rosewood ++
               Original glass fittings +++
               Inlaid decoration +++

ref. **WI820 (351)**

A late Georgian mahogany corner washstand, c.1800, with fretted top to provide carrying handles and drawers below. The price of such pieces often depends on the existence of a set of china bowl and beakers to fit the spaces in the top shelf.

Price Range: £40 – £60

Value points: China fitting set +++
               Decorative inlays and veneers +++

ref. **CL1830 (349)**

A late Georgian mahogany wine cooler or celleret. These pieces of furniture had a lock and were lined with lead, with partitioning for bottles. They were provided with casters and had carrying handles. Various designs and ornamentation were used following period taste up to the Regency period, when they came into general use. They are mentioned by Hepplewhite and Sheraton as well as an illustration in George Hope's *'Household Furniture'* of 1807. and George Smith's of 1808.

Price Range: This example £150 – £200
Value points: Inlays and figured woods +++
*   Colouring and special designs +++*

ref. **DB1840**

An eighteenth century fruitwood dough bin on square legs. A rather specialised 'country' collector's piece which can be very expensive if in early oak with high patination. On the whole, however, these pieces are not terribly expensive since they are rather cumbersome as television stands and not ideal for storage purposes. Usually they are made of elm or oak and can vary considerably in size.
Price Range: £20 – £40

ref. **WN1850**

This piece of furniture, often falling into the general category covered by the 'whatnot' heading was clearly designed for occasional use in the living or dining quarters of the home. Examples dating from about 1800 exhibit characteristic turned upright supports of the period with perhaps 'bamboo' effects. Later examples go into the less restrained Victorian forms of twist and bobbin turning with turned legs. A drawer underneath is considered a great advantage, presumably to teach baby an early lesson that inquiring little fingers can easily be trapped.

Price Range: Georgian/Regency £40 – £70
               Victorian £30 – £60

TOILET MIRRORS

ref. **TM1860**

The toilet mirror, or dressing glass was introduced in England after 1700 and was fairly rare up to about 1740. Early examples, like that shown above, had a shaped mirror similar to wall mirrors, frequently with a gilt edging around the bevelled glass. The uprights could be turned or straight and the mirror could be tilted by a screw action. Under the mirror was either a shaped box made of deal and veneered in walnut, with tiered small drawers, or a miniature bureau with a fall, also veneered in walnut or possibly of a jappaned type like that above of c.1710 date. They are very charming miniature pieces with all the characteristics of larger furniture as far as mouldings, matched veneers and shaping is concerned.

Price Range: Japanned £200 – £300
*   Walnut   £200 – £250*

ref. **TM1861**

A mahogany toilet mirror of c.1750 with a rectangular mirror, having a shaped moulding — or inward point — at the top corners similar to wall mirrors of the period. The supports are straight and tapering with turned finials at the top and there is a gilt surround to the glass. The top of the base shows an ovolo edge moulding and the drawer fronts are concave. The whole mirror stands on ogee bracket feet. Note that the key plate of the centre drawer is a replacement but that there is no pull, whereas the outer drawers each have a small pull or drop handle. This is a normal characteristic of these toilet mirrors. Usually the base box is made of pine with mahogany veneer on the outer surfaces.

Price Range: £50 – £70

Value points: Condition of glass +++ – some specking is desirable to establish antiquity.

ref. **TM1862**

When there is no box of drawers beneath the toilet mirror, it is known as a cheval glass, as above. This example of c.1750 again has straight tapering uprights with turned brass finials at the top. Note that the mirror's top corners are a simple curve in this case, without the inward point of the preceding example and that there is no gilt edging.

Price Range: *£10 – £20*

ref. **TM1863**

A plain rectangular mahogany cheval glass of c.1780 veneered across the mirror frame with a boxwood stringing line around it. The square tapering uprights have no finials and it is probable that these were originally fitted and have been lost. Good reproduction replacements are easily obtained. Where the uprights are square, the cross stretcher on the base, between them, also follows this shape.

Price Range: £10 – £15

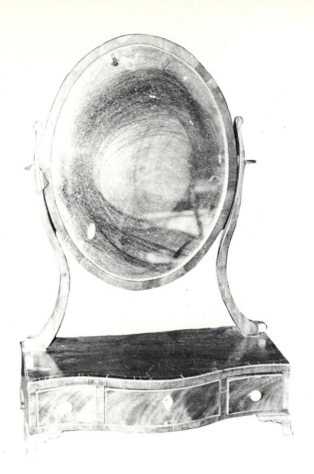

ref. **TM1864**

An oval mahogany 'Hepplewhite' toilet mirror of a type which, with the shield back, has been much reproduced. This one is of c.1785 date and has a mirror frame faced with cross-banded mahogany. The box stand is veneered in figured mahogany and has a serpentine front as well as cross banding around the top. The feet are of the ogee bracket type. The drawers are edged with boxwood stringing and the inset keyhole and outer drawer knobs are ivory. The drawer linings are thin oak. This shape and the shield shape, deriving from chair back shapes of the period, are the most popular of late Georgian toilet mirror purchasers

Price Range: £40 – £60

Value points: *Serpentine front ++*
Figured woods and inlays +++

ref. **TM1865**

A rectangular mahogany toilet mirror of c.1780 with reeded uprights ending in turned finials. The mirror frame is cross-banded with mahogany veneer and has a boxwood stringing line inlaid around the edge. The front of the box is slightly bowed and has the same boxwood stringing line around it, as have the drawers. The bracket feet are of a fairly sophisticated shape associated with the later eighteenth century.

Price Range: £25 – £35

ref. **TM1866**

A later Georgian mahogany toilet mirror of c.1810 with turned uprights to the rectangular mirror. The turning shows the double-beaded or 'bamboo-ed' effect beloved to the period. The front is bowed in a later shape from that originally introduced c.1780 and the ivory inlaid keyhole has been replaced later, due to damage, by another wood. Although the box carcase remains deal, the drawer linings are mahogany of a plain grain. The veneers are highly figured and there is a dark stringing line around the drawers and top edge. The frame is again cross-veneered in mahogany and the mirror stands on ball feet.

Price Range: £20 – £30

Value points: Figured woods and inlays ++

N.B. It is interesting to note that turned uprights are not popular in the trade. Many a quick transition to square uprights has been made in order to enhance price.

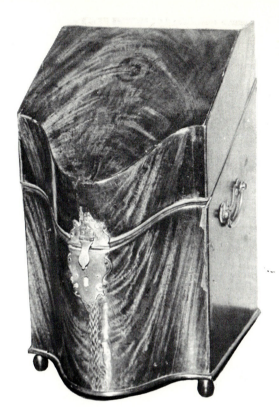

ref. **TB1870**

Knife boxes were originally designed for use on sideboards in the dining room. Knives were expensive and were kept locked in these boxes after being washed in situ. The mahogany example above of c.1790 date is in nicely figured veneer with original lock and carrying handles. Usually these boxes were produced in pairs and it is important that the interior fittings remain intact. Lacquer examples were also produced but mahogany is the more common form.

Price Range: £25 – £35

Value points: Pairs ++++
  Lacquer +++
  Inlays ++
  Silver fittings ++++

N.B. Without interior, price range is £8 – £12

ref. **TB1871**

A mahogany knife box of c.1795 with figured veneer and inlaid shell decoration on the lid. The edges of the box are cross-banded and inlaid with boxwood and ebony stringing in the Sheraton style. In fact Sheraton included knife boxes in his *"Drawing Book'*. Apparently they were a specialist production and not made by regular cabinet makers. The top plate on the lock is missing.

Price Range: £25 – £35

Value points: Pairs ++++
  Lacquer +++
  Inlays ++
  Silver fittings ++++

N.B. Price range without interior £8 – £12

ref. **TB1872**

The interior of the knife box of the preceding example in mahogany, c.1795. The shell and inlaid boxwood and ebony stringing decoration are repeated inside the lid and around the interior fitment edges. It can be seen that the cutlery involved could be stood up inside the box and held in place by this fitment.

Price Range: £25 – £35

Value points: Pairs ++++
Lacquer +++
Inlays ++
Silver fittings ++++

N.B. Price range without interior £8 – £12